Tales From a Design Office

Godfrey Ackers

Pen Press

© Godfrey Ackers 2010

All rights reserved

No part of this publication may be reproduced, stored in a retrieval system, or transmitted in any form or by any means, without the prior permission in writing of the publisher, nor be otherwise circulated in any form of binding or cover other than that in which it is published and without a similar condition including this condition being imposed on the subsequent purchaser.

First published in Great Britain by Pen Press

All paper used in the printing of this book has been made from wood grown in managed, sustainable forests.

ISBN13: 978-1-78003-005-0

Printed and bound in the UK
Pen Press is an imprint of Indepenpress Publishing Limited
25 Eastern Place
Brighton
BN2 1GJ

A catalogue record of this book is available from
the British Library

Cover design by Jacqueline Abromeit

DEDICATION

I have great pleasure in dedicating this book to all those who started work on a drawing board and who might have thought that they were so unappreciated as to have been under it, to those whose confidence could be related to the hardness of their chosen pencils as they sharpened them to the chisel or point, to those who on their first visit to site learnt the value of the boot jack for their mud-caked boots and whose wet and cold hands eagerly clasped the enamelled tin mug of tea, to those who found that a setting out peg was akin to a hedgehog as an invitation to lorry and plant drivers, and especially to those seasoned construction staff who gave their willing help and advice and who kept their tempers when all about them were losing theirs. Above all it is to the long suffering parents, landladies, partners or spouses who sent them off and welcomed them home.

CHARACTERS APPEARING IN THIS BOOK

Consulting Engineers
Noplay & Partners
Sir Triard Tunnelle - Partner
Lady Sylvia Tunnelle, his wife
Ronald Green - Associate
George Plate - Senior Engineer,
Laura - secretary to George
Jim Culvert - student then graduate engineer,
Ahmed - draughtsman
Miss Firesmoke - company secretary,
Vernon Mason - design team leader
Reg - design engineer, short, tubby,
Doodoo - office tea lady,
Moore an old design engineer
Euan Fairway -Manager Scottish Office
Brian Sheet - design engineer
Frances Sheet, his wife
William Bridgeman - Engineer's
  Representative (ER) Triloughs
  Hydro Scheme
John Dicker - a candidate
Sheila - his wife
Ed. - Hydraulics Engineer
Cotton - Hydrologist
Robert Noble - ER Reservoir
John Jewel - site engineer
Jack Paul - engineer
Mackilroy - Section Engineer,
Stanley - Assistant Resident Engineer
  (ARE) Triloughs Hydro Scheme
Janet Dropshot - engineer, various postings
Alec Roadstone, Inspector of Works

Laurel - Architect Adviser

Clients
Firth Regional Council
Chairman
Iain Astare - Chief Engineer

Firth District Council
Ian Astair - Chief Engineer
Architect & Planning Officer
Milroy - Accountant

Achnapond Harbour
John Donovan - Harbourmaster
Jack Lemon - Customs & Excise

Westshire Rural District Council
Chairman - New Works
Estelle Humphrey Jones - Councillor
Sid Blander - Resident Engineer (RE)
Clerk to the Council

Scottish Distilleries
Clare McNash - General Manager
Murdo McStiller - Manager, Glen Kirk
  Distillery

City & County of Southwester
Mr Gidrock - City Engineer
Assistant City Engineer (ACE)

Contractors
Allwork Ltd & MacAllwork Ltd
Peter Oliver Michael Pharaoh - Director, aka Pomp
Harry Smart - Contract's Manager,
    aka Flash Harry

Chief Estimator aka Chief
Alistair McNutt - Site Agent
Mr. Plank - Quantity Surveyor (QS)
Eric - foreman
Doreen - surveyor
Kevin - chainman
Ted Robinson - Agent
Thickear - labourer
Bill - pile driver
Evans - Agent

Advisers to Allwork Ltd
Kinsey - Consulting Engineer
Cambourne - Mining Engineer
Simon Callow - Construction Adviser
 (ex Scottish Ferries)

Wildigrite Ltd
Mackilroy - engineer (Ex Noplay & Partners)
Pit Boss

Other Professionals
Arbitrator
Counsel
Nigel Chesterfield - District Engineer,
 Firth Region Railways
Simon Callow - Scottish Ferries

FOREWORD

The incidents and anecdotes related in this book reflect the time spent by the author in UK while working for firms of consulting civil engineers. They occur during the two decades following the end of World War II and the passing of the Rural Water Supply and Sewerage Act. The technical content is intended to be illustrative, not obtrusive, and what there is of it, it is hoped, will be readily understood by the reader. Fortunately, the Health & Safety at Work Act 1974 had not then been enacted to dominate procedure. Chartered civil engineers at the time were well aware of their duty of care.

The characters are, perhaps, to some extent archetypal. Their names are not intended to relate to those of actual people. The experiences of the characters in this book have, of course, been derived from the author's imagination based in many cases on what memory he has left of actual events, ill-remembered, embellished or adjusted as the case may be. If any persons should think that they recognize themselves in a derogatory light, the author humbly apologises and asserts that it is unwittingly coincidental.

The author gratefully acknowledges all the comments received from a variety of people on bits of the draft, notably members of the Plymouth Waterfront Writers. Especially, he thanks his wife who, apart from bearing with fortitude his occupancy of the computer, helped enormously with her comments.

CHAPTER 1

MY CONSTITUENTS

In Lady Sylvia's upmarket kitchen, Sir Triard Tunnelle, Senior Partner of Noplay & Partners, is getting ready to go to the office.

Sylvia. Well, Triard, if you've got so much new work coming in, how are you going to cope?

Triard. Funny you should ask that. We are starting to try and recruit experienced staff, but its not easy, because we need people with hard living experience overseas. As well as that, the partners have agreed to start taking on university graduates, and Ronald Green is at this moment starting a milk run to universities with good engineering departments.

Sylvia. What that old woman! And he's an awful snob to boot.

Triard. Yes, I know, but he's getting close to retirement and we've put him in charge of the Personnel department, where he'll be able to complete the Times crossword in relative peace. Also he can be an inverted snob, and although he might miss a few potentially good candidates, those he chooses will be OK.

Sylvia. Put off some, you mean. Any how, what's with this Personnel department, what happened to the Staff department?

Triard.   We're having to move with the times and use longer words.

Sylvia.   You'll soon be having to call it Human Resources or such like!

Triard.   I expect you are right dear, but I must be getting off. Where's my umbrella? That's another thing, it needs mending.

Sylvia.   So do three others. Now be off and have yourself a good day.

Triard.   Ugh.

He leaves.

* * * * *

In a sparsely furnished interview room in a red-brick university, Ronald Green and George Plate interview a rather tense Jim Culvert.

Ronald.   Now, Mr Culvert, I have spent some ten minutes describing our firm and its activities.

George   *sotto* Fifteen

Ronald.   What we do now is to spend a few minutes finding out about you and what your ambitions are and then finish up with any questions you may wish to raise. We have had your tutor's report which is good with an expectation of a good

	degree, which we hope you succeed in getting. - *pauses, looks at ceiling, pauses and looks at Jim* - Now, Mr Culvert, what does your father do?
Culvert.	He's head of the Council's out-door sewer teams.
Ronald,	*taken aback.* Hm. Ha! George, he's seen work at the sharp edge. Very good.
George.	He would certainly be starting from the bottom up.
Ronald.	Now, Mr Culvert, you can ignore that; this is a serious business. Let's see, what do you expect to be doing in five years time?
Culvert.	In five years, sir?
George.	Don't worry, relax, your life does not depend on your answer. It wasn't until a few years ago that I realized what I really wanted to do.
Culvert.	What was that, sir?
George.	Retire.
Ronald.	Now, Plate - *Ronald is a surname man with colleagues* - levity won't help, but Mr Culvert, Mr Plate is right up to a point. Let's take things in more order. Are you at this interview merely to get experience of being interviewed?
Culvert.	No, sir, but the course was most interesting and

I thought that an engineering career would be right for me, but only having had some rough experience in vacations with a contractor on a building site, I thought I ought to find out a bit about the consulting side, and this seemed a good way start.

Ronald.   Good. And what tentative conclusion have you reached?

Culvert.   *hesitantly.* My problem is that until I have real experience I can't tell.

George.   Naturally, but explore a bit.

Culvert.   Yes, that's it. It would be nice to get an appointment where different aspects are experienced; design, site work and investigation perhaps.

Ronald.   We do, for promising candidates, make appointments under agreement where we try, as workload permits, to give graduates the experience required by the Institution of Civil Engineers for corporate membership. Is that what you are looking for?

Culvert.   Yes that would be it, and I would like the opportunity to work abroad.

Ronald.   Interesting, and why do you say that? You'll remember from my introduction that the firm has a good presence overseas ...- *the interview continues.*

* * * * *

Some months later in a London tube train, Jim reads his letter of appointment for the umpteenth time telling him to report to Ronald Green, Room 14 on the 3rd floor. When the train stops at St James's Park station he gets out and walks through typical London street scenes towards the office. He wonders what life would be like living and working in London.

At the office. There is an old fashioned entrance lobby and lift. The lift has two, lazy-tong style, steel mesh gates. A young Asian gentleman stands by the button panel. Jim enters and waits a moment.

Ahmed. Good morning, sir. I'm Ahmed. This is my first day at the office. I was interviewed in Pakistan and I'm going to be draughtsman.

Culvert. Well, I'm Jim Culvert and I've had my interview and am coming to start work.

Ahmed. Ah. And very good luck to you, too.

Culvert. OK, so what are waiting for?

Ahmed. *pointing.* You see it says "Capacity - 8 persons".

Culvert. How long have you been in England?

Ahmed. One day, sir.

Culvert.   O.K. We don't have to keep that rule over here, so let's get going. Please shut the gates and press 3 for me.

* * * * *

The building is somewhat like a miniature prison with a central square stairwell balustraded with old wrought iron railings against the well and rooms leading off the landing at each floor. Jim finds Room 14, knocks, and enters at the command given in the well rounded well remembered sonority of the interviewer.

The office has one large desk and usual cabinets, shelves etc. On the wall behind the desk is a large peg board. Jim, slightly nervous, watches Ronald consider a Times crossword clue and enter the answer - in ink; what confidence!

Ronald.   Sit down Culvert, I see you managed to find your way here; to start with, please fill in these various forms. You may find some of them repeating some of your early application forms, but don't worry, there is a system.

Jim gets down to it and finishes them while Ronald returns to the Times crossword.

Ronald.   What on earth are you staring at?

Culvert.   Your peg-board, sir. Most disconcerting trying to get the right hole coinciding with the right hole if you see what I mean.

Ronald. Yes, I think I do. You're not the first person I've noticed staring. Anyhow, you're going to Vernon Mason's design office, but meantime I will show you round the offices and introduce you to some of the worthies whom you ought to be aware of from the start.

Ronald, followed closely by Jim, tours the office. This, in their respective rooms, includes two of the partners, the librarian who doubles as post clerk, one or two specialists who have rooms to themselves, the draughtsmen and tracers (all women), the typing pool and last but no means least Miss Firesmoke:

Ronald. This is Miss Firesmoke, the company secretary, without whom it would be difficult to function, and Miss Firesmoke, this is the Mr Culvert who is starting today.

Firesmoke. Good morning, Mr Culvert, and welcome. You should know that I keep the economies of the office in order, issue consumables and lend equipment, both against a signature. I provide rail tickets and when absolutely unavoidable reimburse expenses against vouchers countersigned by a senior engineer.

Ronald. There you are, you are duly informed, …and warned.

They leave Miss Firesmoke and enter a design office. This room has a large steel wardrobe, filing cabinets, a sort of umbrella-cum-hat stand, a plan chest, four double benches back to back, each about 8 feet (2.5m) long. One half of each bench has half a dozen wide shallow drawers. The other half has a drawing board and T-square on it and space under it for legs, cycle capes, lunch bags, sports gear etc. There is also a desk at which Vernon sits when not prancing about the room or out of it. Two of the benches are occupied by young engineers who look up inquisitively.

Ronald.   Ah. Vernon, I've brought someone to help. This is Jim Culvert. Jim, this is Vernon Mason, one of our design engineers and team leader *they shake hands*; perhaps you can introduce him to the others and show him where to work and get him started.

He leaves importantly, the Times under his left arm.

Vernon.   This is Ahmed the team's new draughtsman. Ah. I see you've met already, and this is Reg an engineering assistant. He's in difficulty, dieting to reduce his circumference and exercising to increase his height, particularly reach. He'll help you to get settled. The problem is that we've got a bit of a panic on. George, that's Mr Plate, has had to go abroad. I've taken his place and you've got to finish what I was doing while I pull the documents together. The firm has promised our clients to get the scheme to tender by Christmas - for God's sake why always Christmas or Easter, why not the end of January or February? It includes some main sewers and a sewage disposal works. It all has to be ready for an official opening a year and a bit from now.

Vernon took Jim up to the third bench, which had one of those tallish bar stools with well worn stretchers to rest feet on and a slit padded seat. It was clearly the worst of the four in the room.

Jim. Why's that?

Vernon. Well, the works serve bits of two parliamentary constituencies and our clients, the two councils concerned, decided it would be nice to have their respective MPs do the opening, and that's the only date the two can make it together. We've allowed 6 weeks for tendering and 12 months for construction, which give about 6 weeks for the usual buggeration factors. So we'd better get on with it….Well, this is what you have to do. This is a humus tank. It's sometimes called a final tank, the last one before final discharge. I've done the hydraulic design and given notional concrete thicknesses. You have to design the reinforcement and fix final thicknesses. You have got to design for two conditions - against floating when empty in saturated ground and when full with no external hydraulic uplift. Reg here will give you guidance on requirements of design codes.

A tea lady enters pushing a trolley.

Vernon. Doodoo, just in time to meet our new recruit; this is Jim Culvert who is anxious for tea and biscuits.

Doodoo *to Jim.* Only one biscuit. That is Miss Firesmoke's orders, but if you're nice to me and someone is

Culvert.   away at the time I might be able to let you have another - if the others don't fight for it.

Culvert.   I'll hold you to that, but why Doodoo?

Vernon.   As you can see, Doodoo is an absolute gem. Flattery should get me everywhere, and, perhaps another biscuit - no, ah well. She got her name when George was in residence. George was a concentrator - also father to a child just beginning to speak. He had vaguely noticed that the trolley had come in but had not registered getting his drink. He had half looked up and said: "Where's my doodoo?", whereat Doodoo had said: "Here it is, darling." so Doodoo she was from then on.

Reg shows Jim a typical reinforcement drawing of a similar circular tank:

Reg.   What you do is take a typical section, say a foot (300 mm) wide - calculate the main reinforcement and concrete thickness - draw in one of the bars and show the others by short lengths at the designed centres to stop filling up the drawing with too many lines, then show the distribution steel in accordance with the Code of Practice, this one, CP114.

Jim starts reading the Code of Practice.

* * * * *

Some days later. Vernon looks at the progress Reg had made with his drawing of aeration channels - lots of long parallel lines fairly close together. Vernon goes through the roof.

Vernon. These lines are not parallel. Can't you draw straight parallel lines? You'll have to do it again.

Reg. But Vernon, I can't reach the top end of the board and draw accurately, so when the bottom half was drawn I turned the board round. The T-square can't be square.

Vernon. Clot! Don't blame the T-square. The lines would still be parallel; unless you used the wrong edge of the board. Did you?

Reg. No. Honestly, I didn't.

Vernon. Well, it must be your set square. Better get another one - at least that's your problem, you won't have to go to Miss Firesmoke for it.

Jim. Vernon, please. - *Vernon nods* - Look, Vernon, there are no drawing instruments for me, so I have been borrowing them. Reg says I have to get my own. Is that right, because they are not cheap?

Vernon. Yes, I'm afraid he is, but you don't have to go the whole hog to start with, just a couple of set squares, pencils and so on. You won't be doing anything in ink; that is what the tracers are for.

A week passes.

Vernon. Jim, I'm ready for your drawing to take off the quantities - better still, you take off the quantities while I get on with the spec. Reg will explain the practice on quantities. Now, let's just check your drawing and calcs. Ah, how many of these long ¾ inch (19 mm) bars are there and how long are they?

Jim. About 150 equal to half the diameter of the tank less concrete cover at the edge. They alternate with shorter bars on the outer half.

Vernon. Good. But as I see it, all the long ones seem to go through one spot at the centre of the tank. How are you going to fit them in? Come on, sort it out and get a move on - we're running late.

* * * * *

Just before Christmas, the office conference room has been decorated and the Christmas party is in full swing.

Vernon. Well Jim. How's it going? Well, we got the documents back from the printers yesterday and the tender advert was published today. We've allowed two weeks for applications, which means about 2 days for the average contractor's estimator after he's got out of the New Year's haze! Ah well! here goes: cheers. Jim, you'd better go off and chat up Miss Firesmoke. She looks a bit lonely. - *Jim weaves his way to Miss Firesmoke.*

Jim. Happy Christmas, Miss Firesmoke.

Firesmoke.   Thank you, Mr. Culvert, but I'm going to have to spend time doing the end of year accounts.

Jim.   Well, don't worry about it now. Can I get you another drink?

Firesmoke.   Well, that's very nice of you; could I have a port and lemon, please?

He gets it and returns.

Jim.   That's a very nice chain round your neck, isn't it. Do you think that if I pull it, Miss Firesmoke, you will flush?

Firesmoke.   Don't be rude. Go away, I don't want to speak to you again until you have learnt some manners.

Jim.   Oh! I am sorry, but please don't be like that.

Firesmoke.   Just go away

Just after the party, the design team is preparing bar bending schedules and last minute additional detail before breaking up for Christmas. An older man, Moore, close to retirement, is drawing a somewhat elaborate detail of wrought iron work for some entrance gates, when Triard enters.

Triard.   Happy Christmas everyone and I hope that you will return the second day after Boxing Day,-- and in full soundness of mind and body.

All.   And the same to you, sir.

Triard goes to stand behind Moore and looks over his shoulder.

Triard. Well, Moore, the sheep will love rubbing their arses against that, and Vernon, you will need to keep the pressure on the successful tenderer to keep to the contract programme, and Jim, never refer to the contract period.

Jim. No, sir,

Vernon. Why not, sir?

Triard. That is, unless you really mean it, because the contract period has not elapsed until all obligations are performed. What is normally meant is the time for completion; maintenance, claims and so on can go on for years after that before the contract can be truly considered complete.

On which note he leaves, and Moore looks discomforted.

* * * * *

Soon after Christmas, Vernon is summoned to the Senior Partner's office and waits a minute or so.

Triard. Now, Vernon. Thank you for your report on tenders and draft letter to the successful tenderer, which seems fine. I discussed it over the phone with both clients yesterday to save time, and they agreed, so I got it typed and sent off yesterday. But do you have any reservations?

Vernon. No, sir. I did the analysis late on Friday, and have not had any second thoughts over the weekend. There was nothing out of ordinary with Morework's rates to suggest claims consciousness and, as you will have read, no reservations. Morework & Co. is a small contractor but quite well known, as you know, and has a reasonable reputation.

Triard. Then what do you make of this letter from the second tenderer, Allwork Ltd?

Vernon reads it.

Vernon. Well, it looks as though Allwork has spotted a decimal error in their tender which they wish to correct by reducing their item for preliminaries from £8,000 to £800. Ah! I see the problem; it puts them as the lowest, but we can't take it into account now after the due date for receipt, can we?

Triard. Strictly speaking, and according to the instructions for the tender, we cannot. BUT two things worry me. Firstly, how will the clients react and how will the selected tenderer react if we try to withdraw our letter of acceptance; and, much more importantly, has there been a leak?

Vernon. Surely, that's hardly likely. Someone would have had to go into the design office and look in my top drawer. Although it's not locked; indeed, it's not lockable. - But what about your office?

Triard. I always lock the office door, before going home. Anyhow, I took your report home to read on the train. Leave it with me; I'll have to think how to play this. But the partners may have to think about security in future; we just cannot risk sensitive leaks of tender prices. - *There is a knock* - Now, what? Come in.

Miss Firesmoke enters.

Firesmoke. I'm sorry to interrupt, Sir Triard, but this letter has just come in by special messenger, and I thought you would want to see it immediately, as it's from Morework & Co. and answers a letter of yours yesterday.

Triard. Very good, Miss Firesmoke. Let's have a look at it. No, that's all. Miss Firesmoke, but I may need you later. - *Miss Firesmoke leaves, and he reads and gasps and hands it to Vernon - pause -* Well, that seems to let us off the hook; at least, I think so. What do you think?

Vernon. Well, I think that it would be unreasonable to hold them to their tender with their only construction director dead or dying. As the Allwork tender is now the lowest, and was the second tender in the first place, there would seem no obstacle to accepting their corrected tender - and serve them right if there's been some shenanigans.

Triard. It looks that way, and there's no need to consider the possibility of a leak or to let the idea surface anywhere. Right? Nevertheless, I must inform the clients of the change and its circumstances, advising that it would be risky to force the contract onto the original lowest having regard to the loss of their one important experienced director.

* * * * *

Meanwhile, in the Director's office of Allwork Ltd, the civil works director is meeting with one of his contract managers and his chief estimator.

Old Pomp. Well, Flash, you'll have heard that our offer of a reduction seems to have done the trick. I'm not sure that it's totally on the up and up and I rather expected Triard to reject it. But who's complaining? Well done Chief, your first estimate was pretty close. - *Goes to drinks cabinet* - What'll you have Harry, Chief?

Flash and Chief in unison. Large G & T please.

An office boy enters and hands a magazine to Old Pomp.

Old Pomp. Good, here's the Contract Journal. Should give some details. - *He flips through the pages with one hand, getting bottles out with the other* - Bloody hell - *he puts the bottles away* - It says here that Morework & Co.'s was the lowest tender but have gone into administration. Damn and blast! That's £7,000 down the drain!

Flash.	Now, who are we going to have for Agent? He'll need to be a good claims' man.
Chief.	Well, what about - *the discussion continues.*

* * * * *

It is now the middle of May and construction of sewers and sewage works is well in hand. Sewers are being laid, the site of the sewage works is taking shape, earthworks and foundations for the structures are fairly advanced, men with tanned torsos stand by while machines work. The usual selection of portable cabins stands near the entrance, one for the site staff lavatories with two compartments, one for the resident engineer's staff and one for the contractor's Agent and his staff. There is an office for each and a small hut at the entrance for the pay clerk who doubles as checker for materials coming in. Were it not for a safe, and the girth of the pay clerk, it looks as though it might easily blow away. Traffic is routed through to an exit the other side of the site.

In the Resident Engineer's site office, Janet Dropshot (the Resident Engineer (RE)) is talking with Alec, the site inspector, who assists her in checking work against the drawings and so on. She is about thirty years old, or maybe a bit more, good looking and obviously fit. He is in his mid fifties and exudes common sense and know-how; he tends to look upon himself as a sort of protective father figure for Janet.

Janet.	Now, Alec, the sewer we're building goes along here, near the road.

Alec.   Yes, miss, and they've just started here - pointing at the drawing. *There's a knock and the Agent enters.*

McNutt.   Sorry to barge in, Janet, that's just what I wanted to talk about. Please let Alec stay. That bit of common has got a large pond on it just where the sewer crosses it, and its not shown on the ordnance survey map.

Janet.   So?

McNutt.   So, I shall want an extra on the rate for the part that crosses the pond.

Janet.   Well now, let's look at the Contract, shall we? How long would you say the pond has been there?"

McNutt.   The locals say for some years, but no-one can go farther back than 5 years. But that's not the point. The Ordnance Survey map has not been revised to show it.

Janet.   Sorry, Alistair, that is just the point; you see the fool of the Contract at Clause 11 says that you shall have inspected the site, and Clause 12 says that you shall have satisfied yourself as to its nature and sufficiency of your prices - or words to that effect. - *they look at the actual words.*

McNutt.   OK, but the standard method of measurement says that there should be a special item in the Bill of Quantities for Works carried out under water.

Janet. No, Alec, don't go away, we may have something to do. Now, Alistair, I don't know what edition of the Conditions of Contract you are used to working under but you'll see that this contract is under the fourth edition, which is a lump sum contract - quantities for the Works in the Contract have to be priced to cover all costs in the Contract. This sewer is described in the Contract and measured in the Bill of Quantities, and you should, are deemed to, have seen the pond and priced for it. Hard luck, and I'll beat you at squash tonight if you can spare the time.

McNutt. No, I can't, and this is going to the Contracts Manager for a formal claim under Clause 66.

Janet. Sorry, that's premature - see Clause 2. I don't know whether your head office has advised you yet but last week I was made Engineer's Representative (ER), so I am no longer just a Resident Engineer. You now have to go to the Engineer for confirmation or otherwise of my decision. But let's be a bit more constructive. How come this pond and why? Alec and I will investigate. I suggest you try to find out the circumstances in more detail? - *McNutt leaves in a huff* - Alec, got any ideas?

Alec. Well Miss, it looks as though we'd better look and see what we can find.

They put on donkey jackets and knee boots, take the drawing and leave. When they reach the common, they stop and have a good look round the pond and the boundaries of some houses off to one side. They stop on the road where the sewer is to go.

Janet. It took longer than I expected to walk round this pond, Alec. Well I can't see any signs of surface water diversions or culverts which could cause this, but I did see a water board valve chamber some way back there. Do you think there could be a water main anywhere near the pond?

Alec. Don't know, Miss, but we could soon find out.

Janet. How? I'll bet the water company's records are not all that brilliant, round here anyway.

Alec. Haven't you done any dowsing? No? Oh well, it's dead simple. I'll show you how, but you'll look a bit silly. - *He looks around and finds an old wire coat hanger at the edge of the pond, straightens it, bends it into an arc and holds each end lightly between the thumb and forefinger.* - Look. We'll walk over to near the valve box, and traverse until we pick up the main. - *They do this. Alec walks steadily with his hands and the wire in front of him looking into the far distance, until suddenly the wire dips.* - Come on, you have a go, Miss. See if we can trace the main.-

Janet took up the wire, and after a bit of practice gets it working to her delight. They are able to trace the main which runs along the edge of the pond to the group of houses on the other side of the common. At one point the wire seems to dip more or less anywhere.

Alec. I'll bet there's a fracture here somewhere.

Janet and Alec return to the office and take off their outdoor clothes. Janet picks up the phone and dials.

Janet. Ah. Alistair. I'm glad I've caught you. Please come round. *McNutt enters.* Have you come up with anything about the pond? No. Well I think we have. It looks as though there may be a fracture in a water main on the edge of the pond, here.

McNutt. And how did you manage to find that out?

Janet. Oh. Just with a bit of dowsing, you know. Yes, we are rather clever. If you play your cards right, you might get a payment from the water company and be able to build the sewer in the dry if you reschedule it for a bit later.

McNutt. OK alright, alright, there's no need to gloat. OK, and thanks. If it works out, and I don't say I believe you, I'll give you a game tomorrow night and a beer if you beat me.

Janet. Done

McNutt leaves. Janet starts to write up the site diary and Alec puts the kettle on.

* * * * *

Outside the Resident Engineer's office, Janet and the Contractor's Quantity Surveyor (QS), are agreeing the monthly measurement. It is a superfine day, so they sit side by side at a table. Janet is dressed in a reasonably discreet minimum with a white tennis cap and curls. The QS wears open necked shirt, grey flannel trousers with a snake skin belt, and a multicoloured club cricket cap.

Janet.   Did you take up quantity surveying, Mr. Plank, because you were sort of led into it by your name?

Plank.   Uh?

Janet.   You know, Plank's quantum.

Plank.   Oh, I see; No; I first went into the building trade – perhaps 'planks' had something to do with it, and then did some of the site measuring before realising there was a possible career in it, so went to night school to qualify. This is my first job on a civil engineering contract, my last 15 years has been on building works.

Janet.   Interesting. You'll probably find some differences between civil and building contracts. Well, let's get on with it. - *They get on with it. Alec turns up with mugs of tea* – Oh. Thanks a lot Alec, very welcome. Mr Plank, do you play squash?

Plank.   No, only cricket in the summer and skittles in the winter. My brother and I open the batting for Great Wallop.

Janet.   My goodness, two Planks; that must be a formidable opening. - *They work on.*

Plank. Well, that's got rid of everything except the humus tanks. We can get them finished before lunch.

Janet. But they are not billed.

Plank. That doesn't matter. We must agree quantities and rates using similar rates where applicable, just the same as building contracts.

Janet. Let me think. - *looks through the Conditions of Contract* - Well Mr Plank, for the record, I'm prepared to agree quantities with you, but as far as I am concerned this is a lump sum contract, the Contract contained detailed drawings for the humus tanks and a specification relating to them. The rates for other measured work are deemed to cover the price for the humus tanks.

Plank. Come, Miss Dropshot, you can't mean that.

Janet. But I do, and there's no point in pushing it with me, you must go further up the ladder; I'm willing to save time, in case it's needed later, by at least agreeing the quantities. *Plank sniffs, but they get on with it.*

After lunch McNutt enters the Resident Engineer's office after a peremptory knock and before being invited in.

McNutt. Morning. Look, Janet, the QS has told me you're not passing payment for the humus tanks. It's nonsense, you can't do this.

Janet. Oh, yes I can. We've really been through this before with the sewer and the pond.

McNutt. But that was totally different.

Janet. No it isn't. It's the same principle. Look, these are the actual words here in Clause 5 "So far as the necessity for providing the same is specified in" (see the Drawings) "or reasonably to be inferred from the Contract"; and here in Clause 1(g): "Contract means the General Conditions, Specification, Drawings, priced Bill of Quantities ....."; and here in Clause 12: "The Contractor shall be deemed to have satisfied himself.....as to...sufficiency of his tender ... and of the rates and prices stated in the priced Bill of Quantities ..... which shall cover all his obligations under the Contract". and here in Clause 13: ..... the Contractor shall execute, complete... The Works ....."; and finally here in Clause 1(e): "The Works means the works to be executed in accordance with the Contract". There, you see?

McNutt. By God, Miss Dropshot, are you throwing the book at me?

Janet. Of course, Mr. McNutt. Isn't this what it is for?

McNutt. We'll see about that - and the squash is off.

Janet. OK. We'll put it on the Agenda for the next Site Meeting

McNutt. What? The squash? It'll certainly be a bit of a

squash, 'cos I'm bringing the big guns down.

* * * * *

At length, a formal meeting in the Resident Engineer's office is arranged. It is full with the Agent, the QS and Flash Harry for the Contractor, the RE and Vernon Mason for the Consulting Engineer. Alec is in the background. The Contract programme is unrolled and examined in detail.

Flash.   We are confident we can complete in time if you give an extension of time of one week to cover disruption due to repairing the water main for the water company and rescheduling the length of sewer concerned.

Vernon.   Now, Clause 44 says that the Engineer can determine an extension of time if there is extra or additional work or other special circumstance of any kind which may fairly entitle the Contractor to an extension of time. As our ER, Janet, has explained, there is no extra or additional work in the Contract. The pipeline was to be constructed where shown, the pond was visible to a site inspection before tendering. However, I think that the wording about special circumstances is sufficiently wide for me to recommend to the Engineer an extension of one week on account of the repair to the water main – a procedure to which we had no objection.

Flash.   Then you will grant us the extra cost of the time involved.

Vernon.	Oh, no we won't. See **Pearce v Hereford** which fits this situation almost exactly.
Flash.	Don't come the barrack room lawyer with me. I'll take the matter to the Engineer.
Vernon.	OK, that's best. Shall we minute this as a notice of claim under Clause 52(4)? Yes, Janet, what is it?
Janet.	I've already given an ER's decision on the cost aspect, which denies the claim.
Flash.	You're dead right. This is a notice of claim.
Vernon.	Yes, yes; it's so minuted, but can you confirm you can finish in the time for completion plus one week?
Flash.	Yes, yes. Everything else is on programme and we're into summer weather now to complete the outside work. We can do the finishes in the winter.
Vernon.	Good. You are fully aware, aren't you, of the opening date arrangements with the MPs?
McNutt.	Of course. Janet never lets a day pass without mentioning it.
Janet.	There is a tide in the affairs of man which taken at the flood .....
McNutt.	No more floods, thank you.

Vernon.	Come to order. What's the next item?
Alec.	Tea, sir - and biscuits.
Vernon.	Good. Thanks. Ah! More and better biscuits than we get in my office.
Flash.	Doubtless, Janet will have told you about her dispute with our QS on account of the lack of quantities for the humus tanks?
Vernon.	Yes. Doubtless she'll have told you of her reasons for denying it, with which I agree - at least on the face of it. Have you got any more to add to the argument?
Flash.	Yes: One - every structure in the Contract and every pipeline has its section in the Bill quantified in detail except the humus tanks. Absence of a Bill for this is a negligent omission. Two - the Contract refers to the documents in the Contract, which include the priced Bill of Quantities, which it says are deemed to be mutually explanatory. There are no items for the humus tanks so there is no mutuality of explanation possible. Three - we were the lowest tender and our rates for all the other items cannot possibly be construed to cover the cost of the humus tanks. It would be totally inequitable to decide that they do.
Vernon.	Thank you. I do not have the authority to decide on this. There's too much involved, although on the strict wording of the Contract, I cannot see

	that you have much of a case - unfair though it may appear. You see, contracts are not concerned with equity.
Flash.	Possibly not, but what about your negligence in common law! Huh?
Vernon.	I don't think we can carry this much further here; shall I minute that this is notice of another claim, and that you will refer it to the Engineer for his decision under Clause 52(4)?
Flash.	Agreed.
Vernon.	Good. That seems to wrap it up for the day. Will you join me for a beer at the New Inn in about half an hour before I drive back to London? Drinks on me.

Flash, McNutt and Plank in chorus.   Yes, thanks,

And they leave.

Janet.	Vernon, can I have Saturday morning off? The Contractor will only be doing formwork and other Temporary Work.
Vernon.	What for?
Janet.	We're playing an important match away involving a long journey by car in the morning.
Vernon.	Did you win your matches last time?

Janet. Yes. 3 out of 4.

Vernon. OK. Any less than 3 and you won't get approval of the next request.

Janet. You're a hard man.

* * * * *

About six weeks later, Allwork Ltd. receives a letter from the Engineer, and the Director in his office discusses it with his estimator.

Pomp. Chief, just listen to this; it's from the Engineer about the Upem and Downem sewage scheme: "I confirm that I agree with the decision of the Engineer's Representative in disallowing extra payment for the sewer affected by the pond on the common, but in accordance with Clause 44 I agree to an extension of time of one week.

I have given careful consideration to your arguments in support of your claim in respect of the humus tanks, which I have discussed with you and with the Employer. It has been agreed by me and the Employer that there was an accidental omission from the Bill of Quantities and that, had it been included, there would inevitably have been an extra cost to be borne by them. It has been agreed by them, if only to avoid further costs in arbitration and litigation, but particularly in the light of your efforts to complete in time, that I should allow your claim in principle. I therefore decide in accordance with Clause 52 that you

	are entitled to payment for the humus tanks on the basis of the Quantities agreed between your QS and the Engineer's Representative subject to valuation in accordance with Clause 52(1).
Chief.	Well, that's a relief at least, although we could have done with some more from the pond's claim.
Pomp.	Do we go to arbitration on the pond claim? I think not; its not worth the effort.
Chief.	Or the risk - only the lawyers would win anything worth talking about.
Pomp.	Huh! I wonder how much of his fees he had to cough up for his negligence! Let's have a drink. What's yours?

* * * * *

Back at the site, the day before the opening arrives, and in her office Janet discusses final arrangements.

Janet.	Alec, have you got the hose connected up to the discharge at the outfall and discreetly hidden?
Alec.	Yes, Miss, yeah, its all OK. Some work still needs to be done in the marquee, but its coming on. Lets hope it don't rain.
Janet.	And the lecterns; you know, sort of raised tables on which to rest their speeches.

Alec.   Right, miss I'll get the chippy to make up two, with a cut out in each for the glass of sewage - should be worth watching!

Janet.   Now, Alec, see that no one gives the game away.

Alec.   Too right.

Next day, people assemble in the open area between the Site offices. They include two MPs, two mayors and their wives, two chairmen of the drainage committees and their wives, the two chief engineers and surveyors and two treasurers with assorted wives, girlfriends and daughters, the 'Engineer' Sir Triard, Vernon Mason, Janet, the Contractor's site staff, Director and Contracts Manager - all looking relatively spruce. There are two lecterns made of 4"x 2" with bits of 7"x 1" to top them. The Engineer goes and stands between them and bangs his umbrella on a shovel.

Triard. Right Honourable Member for East Upem and Member for West Downem, Mayors, ladies and gentlemen. It gives me great pleasure to say that the Contractor has completed the Works to my satisfaction and that a week ago I gave a certificate to that effect. You can see that the Works are operating - *the aeration channels are bubbling away* - and to show that I have full confidence in the design and our supervision of construction I will ask my Inspector of Works to get two full glasses from the effluent outfall. Alec, please go ahead.- *Alec does, gives them to the Engineer, who holds them up, examines them with apparent satisfaction and puts one on each lectern* - I would explain that because these Works serve two parliamentary constituencies, the respective Members of Parliament have kindly agreed to declare the Works open. After tossing coins, the Member for West Downem is to start the proceedings and the Right Honourable Member for East Upem will follow. Sir, the field is yours. - *At this moment, the wind starts to blow gustily, the local aeroplane club starts functioning and traffic noise builds up* - Ladies and gentlemen the Honourable Mr Kevin Hornlea.

He is a somewhat portly man in tweeds. He goes to the stand and makes the usual sort of speech interrupted by noises off, wind in the microphone, poor microphone technique etc., but some of his words are heard.

Hornlea. …the skill of the Contractor and his workmen, demonstrating all that is best in British labour ...- *he takes up the glass, looks at it very carefully. Shakes his head, makes the sign of the cross* - and now, to show my confidence in the skill of the Contractors I drink to the health of my constituents. To my constituents! - *All applaud.*

Triard. Thank you very much, sir. And now, ladies and gentlemen, Sir Marmaduke North will close the proceedings. Sir, over to you.

Sir Marmaduke, dapperly dressed, goes to the other lectern and gives the usual inaudible speech from which in a lull in the wind his words towards the end are heard.

North. And so it is good to see two public authorities cooperating in this joint effort to the benefit of their several budgets and to avoiding the need for two separate sewage works to impinge on the environment. It is also good to see that Britain can continue to follow the tradition of independent professionals and none better than your Engineer. In full confidence in his design I also drink to the health of my constituents. I declare these works open - *He looks heavenward, bows to the assembly, picks up the glass, lifts it high* - FROM my constituents!

And drinks the lot in one gulp. All applaud, laugh and disperse to the marquee except Alec who disconnects the hose from the mains and collects it from the outfall.

CHAPTER 2

YOU CAN'T WIN

It is a Friday, and Sir Triard is preparing to leave home for the office, with homburg, umbrella and brief case.

Triard. Well, cheer-oh, darling. By the way I have to go to Scotland next Monday for a few days, probably leaving Sunday night - thought you ought to know!

Sylvia. Thank you very much, dearest, but your memory is beginning to fail; we are committed to Cornwall all day Tuesday - your favourite daughter's baby is being christened. Remember? *with heavy emphasis* Your first grandchild.

Triard. Damn. I'll have to fix for someone else.

Sylvia. What about one of your partners?

Triard. They'd be no good. Just get up the Scots' noses in no time at all - treat them like colonials.

They peck and he leaves. After he reaches his office he sends for George, who arrives promptly and knocks.

Triard. Come in. Oh. George, good, please sit down - I've got a job for you which I was going to do, but find I can't for personal reasons"

George. Oh! I hope its not bad news.

Triard. On the contrary, no, only recognizing officially another contributor to the sewers. - I want you to go to Scotland on Monday. There are a number of things to do. You can take Janet Dropshot with you; she's recently chartered and between jobs, quite experienced for her age with a good degree and should be able to help. Could be useful for her, anyway, as I'm thinking of posting her there.

George. The timing is OK with me, and I'll be glad to meet Janet; I've heard quite a bit about her - sporty type I believe.

Triard. Yes, and a little better read than some I could mention. But don't let that interest you; she's got something going in a stand-off sort of way with the agent on her last job - happens to be in Scotland at the moment.

George. Sir, Sir, I'm married. But we're not match-making I hope, sir; anyhow, what have we got to do?

Triard. Firstly, we have been retained by both the Firth Regional Council and the Firth District Council to advise on some contractual claims; so you'll need to visit a sewer site to have a look as one of the claims is about it. At the same time on behalf of the Hydro-Board I want an inspection of the portal on the exit of the tail race tunnel, which happens to be near-by; at the same time it would be as well to look at the exposed lengths of penstock feeding the hydro station for condition etc. so that I can alert the Hydro-

Board if necessary. - *George starts taking notes* -. Next, try to fit in a visit to meet the Whisky Distilleries Ltd's manager in Glasgow about a possible job at their Glen Dirk distillery. If you play your hand right, you might get the job and start on it straight away. Also, you'll have to see the Firth Region's Architect Planner about the siting of a pump station and water tower. It looks like at least two days, certainly three if you go ahead on the distillery job. You'd better plan for three and go by overnight train on Sunday and hire a car. Our local man can organize it - and hotels. He's Euan Fairway - know him? - *George nods negatively* -. While you're doing all that, Janet can go North to meet the contractor and a rep. from the Regional Council - her old enemy and friend - to advise on claims. You'd better join her on Wednesday and sort out any final points before introducing Fairway to the local railway man about putting a water main under the line. Incidentally, Fairway has got a bit of a stammer - mostly more or less under control - anyhow he's fixed up the meeting.

George. Sounds like a full trip, sir; I'll get Janet to fix up rail tickets etc. with Miss Firesmoke, while I read up the files.

Triard. OK George, good luck - call in when you get back.

George leaves and goes to the design office where all desks are full. Everyone is beavering away, with Ahmed, the draughtsman, talking to Vernon about drawing layouts and programming them.

George. Vernon, sorry to interrupt, but can you get Janet Dropshot to come and see me, and then show me where the files are on our Scottish work. Who is this guy, not seen him before?

Vernon. Oh! this is a new graduate engaged while you were abroad - James Culvert - he's reading up the new Code of Practice for concrete.

George. How do you do? Settling in well, I hope? Question everything. Routine can lead to mistakes. These new so-called Codes OF Practice are not like the old ones which were about established tried and tested practice; these new ones should have been called Codes FOR Practice, largely dreamed up by academics.

He turns.

Jim. Any chance, sir, of getting a posting to site. It could help me get things into perspective, now that I've been here for nearly 5 months?

George. Good idea. You're under agreement I believe. I'll see what we can do when I get back from Scotland - Ah! there you are, Janet.

Jim. Thanks.

He gets down to his studying, assiduously making notes.

Janet enters - dressed up as befits the London office, not down as for a construction site. The tea lady follows her with trolley.

Vernon. Well done, Doodoo, just in time to feed the boss and his lady friend.

Doodoo. Here's your Doodoo, sir, and yours, miss; don't you let him get away with anything - he's married with a young child who likes his Doodoo.

Janet. What, no coffee?

Doodoo. Now, now, we're not the Ritz you know.

She continues to distribute tea and biscuits.

Vernon. Look, Doodoo, George is away for a few days - can you save his biscuit for me, please - chocolate digestive if possible?

George. Janet, good timing. - *they shake hands* - Now, we're going to Scotland by overnight train on Sunday, back by Wednesday night train. Can you make it?

Janet. Well, I had organized a squash match for Tuesday - I suppose I could cancel it - cost me a beer or two.

George. Yes. You'll be with me on Monday doing some inspections, so take some rugged shoes. - *looking at her smart courts* - On Tuesday you'll be on your own further north meeting a contractor about some claims and Alistair MacNutt of the Firth Regional Council.

Janet.   Oh! No problem about cancelling my match.

George.   Good. I'll tell you more about it on the train when I've read it all up. Meantime, please go and see Miss Firesmoke - know her? I see you do - and organize tickets, sleepers etc and get onto our local man, Euan Fairway, to hire a car and fix hotel reservations.

Janet.   Sleepers? two second class bunks or two first class?

George.   I think we'd better go first class, all things considered - but it might be fun to see how Miss Firesmoke reacts if you suggest the former. OK? See you at the station then.

Janet leaves and George is shown to the filing cabinet and settles down with some files. Janet goes to Miss Firesmoke's office.

Janet.   Sorry to spring this on you at short notice, but Mr Plate has asked me to ask you to get return tickets to Edinburgh for Sunday night, back Wednesday night.

Firesmoke.   They never give much warning, do they? Expect miracles they do. But we always manage it somehow. You'll be wanting sleepers, of course?

Janet.   Yes, please. I know how well you look after the firm's expenses, so perhaps we ought to share a two berth cabin?

Firesmoke. Don't be ridiculous, Miss Dropshot, we're an independent professional firm and that means independent cabins, besides, these costs will be charged to clients. Well I never.

Janet sotto. I bet.

On Sunday evening at Euston station, Janet enters George's first class sleeper, where George had left the door open.

George. Well met Janet, have a little night-cap? I hope your compartment's OK.

Janet. Yes please, yes, fine, its next to this one.

George. Anyhow, I hope you've had a good meal - 11 pm is not the best time to join a train - but - *putting on a Scottish accent-* we can have a wee drop and a short chat before you go to bed. Ever been to Scotland?

Janet. No, this is my first visit - anything I ought to know?

George. Not much that you won't pick up on the way, but perhaps one or two things - I hope you haven't brought a kilt - good, that could have been a serious mistake - only a few words of warning. First, remember that you are entering a different country and behave accordingly with due consideration. For example, they have their own bank-notes. In some respect they are not unlike the French - their legal system for instance, and a tendency to speak in rounded paragraphs unlike our sentences. But even if you can see the end before they get there, for goodness sake don't interrupt or finish it for them; it doesn't do first impressions much good; and don't be too surprised if you find good education at all levels of society. They seem to have got that right where we haven't.

Janet. Well, that was a good paragraph to get on with! But what was that about the legal system?

George. Well, before the Treaty of Union, sometimes called the Act of Union.

Janet. 1707.

George *eyebrows raised* not to be confused with the Married Women's Property Act, the Scottish lawyers used to train in France, and the Scot's law - by the by Scotch is whisky and a Scotchman is a device for stopping a rope or chain from running away - is based on Roman law, and each civil case is in theory found on first principles not as in England and Wales on the precedent set by the most recent relevant case, which though not binding in Scotland is still persuasive, as they say. Sorry, I do tend to go on a bit and you are tired. Finished? Good, sleep well - fortunately we're in the middle of the coach - at the ends the square wheels can be a bit disturbing, especially near the border! We can talk more over breakfast. Have you got a knife or scissors? You'll need some to get

at the biscuit with your morning tea if you're not
to risk finger nail damage.

Janet goes with a wave.

Next morning, Monday, Euan picks them up from the station and takes them to the lower end of the loch. It is a rather drizzly morning, and they stop on a good looking road with no footpath but bungalows and houses on each side with small front gardens. On one side behind the housing is a steeply rising rocky hill; on the other, at the end of short back gardens, the ground slopes down to the edge of the loch. Opposite the last of the houses a trench has been opened up for about 100 m; the nearest 30 m or so has been backfilled and a manhole constructed at each end. Men are working in the trench laying a sewer on gravel, some one and a half to two metres deep, with a back-actor digging the trench ahead of them. George alights from the Landrover and speaks to Janet sitting beside Euan, the driver.

George.   Now Janet, let Euan take you to the portal. I think it's a simple enough job - just see where the drips are coming from and see if anything needs to be done. Remember it can freeze badly up here. Then he can show you the penstocks leading to the hydro station. Have a look at them, and log their external condition and anchorages with any recommendations. OK Euan?

Euan.   Y-yes. J-jjanet you'll nnnhave to wwwear oilskins. There are sssome in the bback.

Janet.   OK George; I've brought a camera which may be useful if the rain does not set in.

George. Good, then we'll meet at the Sporran Arms for lunch, say half past one, because I've a Council meeting at Firth to go to at half past three. You've got a separate car for me, Euan?

Euan. The C-council are sss-arranging one for yyyou to mmmrendezvous at the Sssporran Arms at tttwo.

They drive off. George takes in the scene, looks at the weathered rock sides of the trench which is curtained off from occasional traffic by a striped ribbon attached to steel stakes on concrete blocks very near the trench sides. It provides just enough carriageway for the traffic. He puts on his oilskins and calls the foreman over.

George. What cheer? My name is George Plate, and I'm here to have a look on behalf of the Firth District Council. This doesn't look safe to me.

Foreman. Ooh, I wouldna say that. You ken see the subsoil is very sound.

George. But look, the men are not wearing hard hats, and at this depth you are on the borderline of needing trench supports of some sort. Even if the muck is good quality, this is a bus route, isn't it? and a heavy moving load this near to the trench could set up movement.

Foreman. Well, Flash Harry, that's the Contract Manager, said its OK.

George. Well, I don't think so, but I do not have any

authority in this contract, but as an experienced member of the public I would suggest you do something about it. I'll take it up with the Contracts Manager when I see him on Wednesday.

Foreman. Orlright, if you say so.

George. I do.

Foreman. Well, what do you suggest?

George. For heaven's sake, you're the foreman, you ought to know. But if you want a suggestion, at least get the men to wear hard hats and either support the trench sides or institute traffic control to stop all passage until men are out of the trench. Good thing it's not the tourist season yet. Now, I want to have a look at the pipework and bedding, so please stop the traffic, get me a hard hat and while the men are getting theirs, lets go down and have a shufti - look-see to you.

They climb down and George checks alignments, the depth of bedding and the joints. The bedding is very wet, and freestanding water appears and seems to rise. He raises his eyebrows to the Foreman.

Foreman. Yes, you see, sir, the water level goes up and down with the water level in the loch. It's at the top end of the tidal reach, but not bad enough to prevent work, although actual laying and jointing takes place about 3 to 4 hours each side of low water.

George.   Hm! That's not going to help stability.

He nods; they get out and he goes down the first manhole while the foreman waits at the top. After a little George emerges.

George.   Look here, these segments have not been properly bedded in mortar and are leaking ground water into the sewer. You'll be required to seal them. I expect a Council engineer will come and have a look in a day or two.

A brief rain shower washes the oilskins clean as George starts walking to the Sporran Arms.

At the same time, further up the loch, Janet and Euan inspect the interior of the concrete and masonry portal, which has a stream running down the middle; Janet takes notes and a photo or two; they then climb up round the outside looking at the masonry arch where it is exposed. It's too far away to hear conversation above the noise of the stream and the wind.

Then, outside the portal, Janet and Euan climb a steep hillside down which are two steel pipelines separated by steps and stairs. Again, Janet takes notes and photos from time to time, while Euan points at features to be looked at. Again, distance makes any conversation too difficult to hear. They return to the Landrover and start towards the Sporran Arms. On the way, they overtake George and pick him up.

George.   Janet, this is the sewer about which MacAllwork is making a claim. You might well take a look at it now and catch me up on the way to the pub.

Janet alights with Euan and takes it all in before setting off in the Landrover for the Sporran Arms.

They meet George near the restaurant. The team enter at the rear from a side entrance, Janet and George still wearing oilskins. The manager approaches.

Manager.   I'm sorry, we've stopped taking orders for lunch.

George.   Yes, I am afraid we are later than planned, and as a result I at least am in a terrific hurry. I'm supposed to meet the Council's Works Committee at three, but I think we can do without a proper lunch, but would be very grateful if you could rustle up some sandwiches.

Manager.   Och aye, I think we can run to that.

George.   Before you start running do you mind if we sit down like this, and - *looking at the others for agreement* - we could do with three pints of beer, please.

Manager.   No, that will be alright if you sit at the back here. *He moves off swiftly.*

George.   Well, Janet, how did you get on?

Janet.   Fine, thanks, with Euan's gallant help over the rougher bits. There's quite a bit to consider.

George.   We can consider it on the train back, if you like.

The beer arrives and each sips with pleasure. Then the sandwiches arrive.

George.   That's what I call service – *as he nods thanks to the waitress* – My goodness, that was quick.

He tucks in. While chatting, eating and drinking, a man approaches and interrupts.

Driver.   You'll be the party for the Council, I suppose, – *he looks at his watch* – It's already two o'clock and it takes the best part of an hour to get there.

George nods and starts eating his last sandwich very quickly.

Janet.   George, he tires betimes who spurs too fast betimes, with overfeeding food doth choke the feeder.

George splutters.

Euan.   There y-you are, y-you see.

George beckons the waitress with a sign indicating the need for a bill. She arrives and gives him the bill.

George.   I'm sorry, these haven't any pockets, I'll have to drop my trousers to pay you.

Janet.   You can't take him anywhere.

George.   OK you two, I must dash. Euan will drive you north for tomorrow's meetings - see you on

	Wednesday at the Regional Council's HQ - in the morning?
Euan.	Y-yes, sir, the meeting's timed for n-n-n-nine thirty, and thanks for the l-l-meal.

But George had gone.

* * * * *

George enters the dark oak panelled District Council Chamber. It is filled with tobacco smoke, through which one can make out the various councillors round a table all looking as though they had had a good lunch, much of it liquid, except the Chairman at the head of the table, who veritably twinkles.

Chairman. Er, good afternoon Mr Plate. It is very good of you to interrupt a busy programme to come and see us. It is always a pleasure to meet people from south of the border and to compare our various ways of doing things for our mutual satisfaction, pleasure and benefit. For example, I hear you had to take your trousers off to pay the waitress at the Sporran Arms.

George. Sir! News certainly travels fast up here. I'm sorry I'm a little late, but your driver was fairly careful of my nerves, and it was very good of your Chief Engineer to arrange transport for me.

Chairman. Well, Mr Plate, you seem to have arrived safely, so what have you got to report? You're first on the agenda and when all is done with you, you'll not be needed to stay on for the rest of the meeting and will be able to go about the rest of your business.

George. Thank you, sir, that is very much appreciated. In fact, there are really only two concerns. Firstly the sewer works seem to be going more or less satisfactorily bar some faulty work in sealing the manhole rings, which will need correcting. I've told the foreman, but I do not have any contractual authority over him and will follow it up when I see his Contract Manager on Wednesday; meantime it might be a good idea to send an inspector or clerk of works to watch over the construction for a few days to satisfy you that the contractor is up to the job.

Chairman. Yes; Mr Astair, perhaps you can see to that? Carry on Mr Plate.

George. Yes, sir, you will probably know that your contractor has a small claim in respect of these sewer works and that he is also a contractor for the Regional Council who have a much bigger claim against them. I discussed this with Mr Iain Astare, and he agreed that I could try to sort out your claim at the same time and report back.

Chairman. Yes, yes, that's fine, but Mr Astair can also attend to give appropriate presence, and you can deal with our claim first. Carry on Mr Plate, please.

George. I do not think that the safety precautions on site are adequate and have given the necessary warnings to the foreman and, again, will follow it up with the Contract Manager. – *turning to the Chief Engineer* – It might be a good thing if you could spare someone suitably experienced to go up there to keep an eye on things until it is satisfactory.

Chairman. Yes, Mr Astair you'd better do that now and come back as soon as possible. Could you not visit the site, Mr Plate, as a sort of check on your way north tomorrow evening?

George. I'd rather not, sir. As a member of the public, I might have to do something; and as Mr Ackroyd said 'absence of body is better than presence of mind'; I'd much rather leave it to a person of authority, like Mr Astair.

Chairman. You are probably right. Carry on.

George. Just a minute, sir, before Mr Astair goes, there's one other point. The sewer trench hasn't got very far yet, but it is being cut near the middle of a recently resurfaced carriage way and a good 20 year asphalt one at that. Could not the rest of it be sited out of the carriageway, in front gardens or back gardens or in the foreshore of the loch with rider sewers or drains and only a few connections across the road?

Chairman. Good idea. What do you say, Mr Astair?

Astair. It's not really possible, sir; what with all the fiefs

	and the feus we would not be able to get the unanimous consent we would need for several months, if at all.
George.	But can't you just serve notices under Section 283 of the 1936 Public Health Act?
Astair.	Laddie, laddie, this is Scotland; don't you know you are in a different country now. We work under the Burgh Police Act 1892.
George	*abashed* I'm sorry; I am not very familiar with administrative law in Scotland.
Chairman.	Never mind, Mr Plate, you'll learn; but it has been a valuable meeting and thank you very much for all your comments; we'll look into the roadworks and see what can be done to reduce the damage. Mr Astair will let you know if we want to see you next month. Now off you go and have a good meeting with Mrs McNash.

George goes off with Mr Astair, muttering to him.

George.   The spy network hereabouts seems pretty good!

* * * * *

George is driven to the offices of Scottish Distilleries. George is shown into a room of truly baronial proportions and heavily furnished. It is the room of Clare McNash, the Managing Director. He walks towards the distant desk, looking round with admiration at the paintings and pictures, countryside scenes of the **Monarch of the Glen** variety mixed with photographs of distilleries and parts of them, all working away industriously. Clare McNash waves him to a heavy wooden chair.

McNash. Welcome Mr Plate. I hope that you have had a good journey. - *She looks at her watch* - You'll have had your tea then? Sir Triad has phoned to explain why he can't come to introduce you.

George. It's certainly a great pleasure for me, madam. What can I do for you?

McNash. It's probably just as well that Sir Triard can't come. It's probably too small a matter to engage someone of his dignity and eminence - not to mention his charges, and I am sure from his outline of your experience that you'll have no difficulty. The problem concerns one of our distilleries - the Glen Dirk distillery. The Company has decided as a matter of policy that we ought to ensure that the distilleries of our better known brands should be capable of expanding output by 50%. But Glen Dirk's manager says that he can't see his way to doing this for shortage of a reliable increased water supply. They make a good malt and use water from a peaty field above the factory. Subject to one or two formalities, I'm minded to ask you to take it on? In case we agree and you can, I've made a provisional appointment with the Manager, Murdo McStiller.

He will be ready for you if I confirm tonight. But before we settle on it, I need to know what your charges will be.

George. Thank you very much, indeed. I made a provisional allocation of time tomorrow morning, so that would fit in very well. As to charges, I can't give you a lump sum quotation for this stage of the investigation. There are too many unknowns and it will have to be on a time and expense basis. We normally work on two and three-quarter times basic salary plus out of pocket expenses and any outside specialist charges. Then after you have received our report and recommendations when, if you want us to continue, fees can be negotiated on a different basis.

McNash. That's very satisfactory, except I think that the time charges should be less, say two and a half times basic. Do you agree, and what would that be in pounds, shillings and pence?

George. *thinks and calculates* Well, madam, assuming that I can do all the field investigation in one or two visits, and that the preliminary report does not take more than a day to draft, I'm sure Sir Triard will not object to my agreeing your terms. Our hourly rate is derived from basic annual salary divided by 220 working days of 7.5 hours, to which the multiplier is applied. In my case this works out at - *more calculating* - a total charge of £5.50 per hour.

McNash.	Very good; that's fine by me; we'll call it a deal; you can confirm it in writing when you get back to London. I'll let McStiller know. Meantime, it is past the end of the working day, and as you will have had your tea, why not join me in a wee dram? She takes his acceptance for granted and goes to a super drinks cabinet and pours out two healthy drams. She gives one to George, and says .
McNash.	Och aye, good health.

They move away chatting, and sit down on a sofa.

George.	This is very good, madam, and a good thing I have only a little way to walk to the hotel. If its not impertinent, how is it that you have managed, as-it -were, to break out of the glass bottle? I've not seen any but men, yet, in authority.
McNash.	No its not impertinent and call me Clare now - out of office hours of course. Basically I was in the right place at the right time AND I could drink with the other board members dram for dram and not lose my way!

They continue chatting amiably.

* * * * *

On Tuesday morning, there is a large excavation on one edge of which are three temporary buildings; there are large scrapers, bulldozers etc. working away. The largest cabin is the office of the contractor, MacAllwork Ltd., and in it Alistair McNutt, Flash Harry Smart and Mr Plank are talking.

Alistair. With regard to your two claims, one against us and one against the District Council, the Regional Council has decided to call in an independent consulting engineer to advise it and me, as the Engineer under the contract, on the claim against us so that you will not feel that the Council is using its status to bulldoze you or exert undue influence. I should add that I shall take notes and make my mind up in due course. I hope you do not object.

Flash. No, but this is, of course, without prejudice to our rights under Clause 66 to take the matter to arbitration.

Alistair. Agreed, but I think the Consulting Engineer's rep is here - you may be in for a shock.

Janet knocks and enters.

Janet. Let me not to the marriage of true minds admit impediment.

Flash. *groans* Good heavens, it's you again. Anyhow that's not Shakespeare.

Janet. Hello, again, - *she shakes hands with them and rather more warmly with McNutt - turning to Flash Harry* - Yes it is - the first line of a sonnet, but I fear the rest of it is not really apposite.

Flash. *turning to Mr Plank* You can forget that sewer claim, we've been there before.

Plank. Not so fast, Flash er Mr Smart, - this contract is under the fifth edition, the last case was under the fourth.

Janet. I see that you have expanded to Scotland. How's it going?

Flash. Yes. We thought that we should have a wholly owned subsidiary up here, but put a "Mac" in front of the name of the holding company. We thought it might help - in fact, we have already won two contracts - this one and a sewer contract for the District Council.

Janet. Good. As to the sewer claim, my boss, George Plate, is also in Scotland and has had a word with the Chief Engineer, and, to save time, they agreed that I could discuss your claim with them here, after we have dealt with your claim against the Regional Council, when Mr McNutt can leave. I'll take notes and report to Mr Plate with a view to ironing out any outstanding problems here tomorrow morning, to which you are invited - *McNutt nods* - if you have anything further to say. Is that all agreed?. *All nod.* Good, well let's start with the earthworks claim.

Flash. Now Miss Dropshot.

Janet. Please continue to call me Janet as before.

Flash. OK, Janet, this is a very sizeable claim and concerns under-measurement of fill in embankment round the reservoir. Mr Plank can explain.

Plank. The volume of excavation below original ground level *(OGL)* measured geometrically from the drawings is equal to the volume of fill above OGL measured geometrically, and it is all billed like that in accordance with the CESMM (*Civil Engineering Standard Method of Measurement*). However, the excavated material was originally in a relatively unconsolidated state, but, after compaction as specified in the embankment, there is a considerable shortfall which we have had to make good at considerable expense. He draws a sketch in illustration. We think that we are fairly entitled to compensation.

Janet. OK, I can understand your concern, but where is the contractual argument?

Flash. Briefly, under Clause 13, it was a condition which we could not reasonably have foreseen in the absence of any borehole data which, before tendering, we might have expected to have received from the Council in accordance with the words in parenthesis in Clause 11(1).

Janet. That was very well put Mr Smart - perhaps you have had occasion to say the same thing before. But let's look at the clauses. - *they all look* -We'll overlook for the moment that under Clause 13 it's not what YOU could have expected but what an EXPERIENCED CONTRACTOR could have reasonably expected.

Flash. But we are an experienced contractor!

Janet. Of course. - *turning to Mr McNutt* - What about borehole data, Mr McNutt?

Alistair. As far as I can find out, this location was fixed on just before the tender documents were finalized for issue. No subsoil information was available to the Council at that time and therefore under the same clause the tenderer is expected to have satisfied himself as to its condition. He had plenty of time during the tender period.

Janet. In that case, let's see what the contract has to say. Let's assume that you have given all necessary notices under Clause 13.

Flash. We have.

Janet. Then the amended measurement Clause 57 effectively warrants that the Bill has been prepared in accordance with CESMM, so that's where we have to look? - *coffee is now brought in and distributed* - Hm! better biscuits than we get in London; you can't be doing too badly!

Plank. Yes. - *gets up and brings a copy of CESMM which he opens at Class E, Earthworks* - I quote measurement rule M9 "The volume measured for excavation within borrow pits shall be the net volume measured for filling".

Janet. Promising, but aren't there some general rules to tell us what this means? - *She reads* - Ah yes, here in Clause 5.18 it says no allowance shall be made for bulking, shrinkage or waste.

Plank. Unless directed otherwise by a rule in the CESMM.

Janet. But it is not directed otherwise.

Plank. I think it can be construed that way and is supported by rule M19. If we had chosen to import fill otherwise than from borrow pit - it stands to be measured as the difference between net volume of fill and net volume of excavation. If M9 is ruled against, there seems to be a conflict with M19.

Janet. You may be right, but I don't think so. I think 5.18 controls both. However it might be better to see if Mr Plate can cope better than I can. So let's continue this tomorrow, if you haveanything further to put.

Alistair rises to leave and Janet sees him to the door.

Alistair. Janet, can I meet you at the hotel this afternoon, the Screebrae isn't it, say 5.15, and we could go to Kilrauk Castle for a game of squash? You will have brought your kit?

Janet.   Yes. What a good idea.

Alistair.   Its an interesting old-world wooden court, separated from the castle, with plastered back wall, but otherwise all wood. I'm afraid there are no showers, so I'll get you back to the hotel for one and, perhaps, pick you up later for a meal?

Janet.   I'll look forward to that, and write up my reports meantime this afternoon. - *She returns to the meeting table and a few raised eyebrows* - Now, for the sewer claim?

Flash.   Well, the claim is for trench work affected by tidal water, which is not mentioned in the Bill of Quantities.

Janet.   I don't think that the changed edition affects my conclusions under the earlier contract, but let's have a look. - *She looks* - As I see it, the length concerned was separately billed, its location is readily identified from the drawings and you have priced it after having been deemed to have inspected the site etc. all as before. You could hardly have failed to notice the loch. Its a pity the bill item did not expressly mention the presence of open water, but I don't think it makes any difference to your obligations and liabilities for its cost.- *Plank puts another piece of paper to her; she reads it* - Even so, the new standard method of measurement which was incorporated in the contract by an amendment CCSJC/GN3 to clause 57.- *Plank and Flash exchange looks; Plank gets more*

> *coffee* - does not seem to need special mention of water hazard. But time is getting on. Think about it, and if you have anything to add, please say it tomorrow. - *Janet gets up to leave* - Thank you very much for the coffee - and an interesting discussion. I look to see you again tomorrow, perhaps?

There are goodbyes all round.

Flash. See what I said, Plank, not much hope there, but let's see if we can find anything else in support.

They carry on reading and making notes.

* * * * *

On Tuesday morning, George hires a car and drives to the Glen Dirk Distillery, enters the Manager's office where Mr McStiller was waiting for him. After greetings, they get down to business.

George. Well now, Mr McStiller, can you give me a run down of the system and the problem?

McStiller. Our water comes from springs, Mr Plate, at the lower end of a two or three hundred acre peat field. Two springs are collected and piped to a small holding tank which feeds the factory with water for all purposes. We close down for 6 weeks in the summer when the springs tend to be unreliable for quantity. You see we have to be very careful to maintain the quality of our whisky on which our reputation is based, as you can well understand.

George.   Of course, but are these springs enough for expanding production, otherwise?

McStiller.   Yes and no. Overall they may be enough but it varies from year to year and time to time depending on the weather, you will understand, won't you?

George.   Yes, but what I was getting at was why don't you have a reservoir big enough to even out the variations?

McStiller.   Oh! Mr Plate, we cannot use the stored water for the whisky.

George.   I don't see why not, but perhaps you can explain while we go and have a look at the catchment. Besides what happens when you restart after the summer holiday; presumably you use what's in the tank?

McStiller.   Aye, but its a very small tank and only a wee bit of it, if any, goes for the mash.

They pick up coats and George picks up his case full of sample bottles, and they leave. They pass by the tank, look at it, and George takes a couple of samples, one from the inlet and one near the outlets. They climb to the peat field and view the breathtaking views of moorland and hills beyond. George is puffing a bit. There are three springs, two of which are connected by a sand and gravel trench to a pipe leading to the tank.

George. Well, it looks simple enough to me. Just connect in this third spring. It looks more than equal to each of the other two.

McStiller. No we cannot use that. Mr MacTavish in 1934 said we should never use it.

George. Why ever not, it comes from the same fields?

McStiller. I don't rightly know. But whatever Mr MacTavish said goes.

George. OK. What I think we'd better do is for me to take samples from these three to see what differences there are, if any. I'll get the local public analyst to do a chemical and bacterial analysis, while you, perhaps, could see if you can find out what reasons Mr MacTavish had; fair enough?

McStiller nods, and holds George's case while samples are taken.

At length, George finishes and is waved off in his hired car. He drives to the offices of the Firth Regional Council and is shown to the Chief Engineer's office, which is fairly modern, fairly plush, with a biggish table. Janet and Alistair are already there.

George. Hello you two, good morning. Janet, you're looking very sparkly this morning.

Janet. Just shows what a bit of exercise can do.

George.   Hm!

Flash Harry and Mr Plank are shown in. More greetings. They are introduced to George. They sit down.

George.   Mr McNutt; I hope you don't mind but I've suggested that Ian Astair, the District Council's Chief Engineer comes along so that we can get a sewer claim out of the way before dealing with your earthworks claim. It shouldn't take long.

Alistair.   No, that's fine. I would like to meet him anyhow, and it could be useful - Ah! This could be him.

Janet.   He.

She gets a sharp look or two. Mr Astair enters. More introductions etc.

George.   Order…Now, Janet briefed me last night on the phone so there's no need to go over the ground -

Janet.   and with rainy eyes write sorrow on the bosom of the earth.

George.   - again, and Janet for goodness sake restrain yourself. Now I propose to take the sewer claim first so that Mr Astair can get away. Mr Smart, have you anything more to add?

Flash Harry nods to Mr Plank

Plank. Yes, sir, we've had another look at the standard method and refer you to clause 5.20 'work affected by water', which we did not consider yesterday. It says in effect that where a body of water is near the site it should be identified in the preamble to the bill of quantities and a reference made to the drawing showing surface levels etc. We agree that a drawing shows location but not surface levels or fluctuations, and the preamble is silent on the matter.

He unfolds a drawing and they all look at it.

George. Well, it does show mean spring high and low water levels; surely that's enough?

Plank. It would be, if they were related to the ordnance datum to which the sewers are related, but they are related only to some unstated chart datum; anyhow there is still the omission from the preamble to consider.

George *thinks* Yes. There certainly seems to be a departure from the strict application of the rules. If you wish to pursue your claim I suggest that you write to Mr Astair giving details of your rates for the relevant length and of those for other similar lengths unaffected by loch water. He can take it from there. Is that agreeable Mr Astair, or if you like he can send it to me in London?

Alistair. No, that will be fine. I can deal with it. Well, if that's all, I'll be off. Thank you for your help Mr

Plate, but while I'm here, could I raise with Mr Smart the question of safety precautions on sewer construction? - *he addresses Mr Smart* - I think it would be as well if you visited the site and confirm with the foreman what he should do in the light of Mr Plate's comments to him on Monday. I've got a man there meantime to see that there's no danger to workmen or the public.- *Mr Smart nods* - Right then, good-bye.

He goes.

George. Now what about your larger claim for imported fill; have you got any more to say?

Janet nods to Alistair making gestures of drinking coffee. He presses a buzzer and makes similar gestures to a secretary who enters momentarily.

Flash. Not really, except to mention again the doubt raised by the wordings of rules M9 and M19. Also, it doesn't in any event seem right or fair to deny us recompense. It was not like that under the old green book.

George. You are quite right. I don't know why they changed it - perhaps difficulty of measurement or perhaps of policing lorries which might otherwise have a tendency to go off on a frolic of their own.

Flash. We wouldn't do anything like that, of course.

George. Of course, I wouldn't dream of suggesting it. But

	as to your point about the ambiguity, I think that you and Miss Dropshot were too engaged by the small print to look at the first excavation measurement rule, M1. It is quite explicit 'The quantities of earthworks shall be computed net from the Drawings with no allowance etc.' This admits of no ambiguity. The claim fails. Bad luck - I have sympathy but equity gives way to contract.
Flash.	It's not over yet, Mr Plate; there's a lot at stake. We shall have to consider what other course we can follow; for example to obtain an affidavit from the Council that they never had borehole or trial hole details of the subsoil prior to tender.
George.	That's your province Mr Smart and its certainly not in my competence to deal with it here. Now, we really must get away, pick up Euan Fairway and get to a meeting with the local railway chief, before coming back here after a latish lunch to see the Council's Architect and Planning Officer. Mr McNutt can you make sure that he will keep what was a provisional appointment?

Goodbyes are said all round, and they go out as the coffee comes in. McNutt looks apologetically at Janet, who grins and marks an imaginary point on a score-board.

* * * * *

Having picked up Euan, all three proceed to the railway engineer's office The walls are covered with track lay-outs, schedules, overall plan of the region and pictures of famous locomotives etc. George, Janet and Euan are ushered in. All shake hands and settle down.

George. Very good of you to see us at such short notice, Mr Chesterfield. This is Miss Dropshot who has no specific role in this discussion, but may do in the future.- *She looks askance* - This is Euan Fairway, our resident representative in Scotland who you may not have met yet.

Engineer. *speaking rather slowly and deliberately* Well, Mr Plate, no problem, but what can we do for you?

George. Briefly, the Regional Water Company want to lay a water main to cross your line where it is in embankment, - *Euan produces and unfolds a drawing* - about here. We couldn't find any culvert or underpass near enough to be convenient, so we would like to arrange for the pipeline to be thrust-bored under the embankment.

Engineer. *Each word carefully pronounced* Yes. There are drains each side of the embankment which discharge surface water into a stream some way away.

George. We noticed that, but apart from the distance we want to avoid construction below groundwater level, especially for thrust-boring.

Engineer. *slowly* I understand. There's no problem in principle, but we have plenty of rules and regulations which need to be followed, and timing could be important.

George.   Good. Well this is where Mr Fairway comes into the picture. He will consult you and be responsible for the detailed design in our office up here. If you'll forgive me and Miss Dropshot leaving you to it, we'll leave you with Mr Fairway. Euan, go ahead, please.

Euan.   G-g-g-nice to m-mmeet you M-mmr Chesterfield. C-c-c may we fix a d-d-time for a meeting to d-d consider d-detail.?

Engineer.   Of c-c-course. L-l-lets -l-l-see what's in my d-d- appointments b-b-book.

George and Janet hurry out convulsed.

George.   I never realized Chesterfield was an inherent stammerer - how unfortunate!

George drops Euan and Janet off at the Scottish office and proceeds back to the Firth Regional Offices where he is shown to that of the Regional Architect and Planner.

George.   Thanks for seeing me. I gather that you got Mr Fairway's message.

Architect.   Yes, that's right. So, what's the problem?

George.   I'm here on behalf of your New Works Department who have engaged us for their water scheme for the new development. It will require a small pump station and a water tower, preferably near by. We know where we want to put them,

	but before fixing the site, we would like to get your views. Firstly, do you have anything like the English Town and Country Planning Act 1945?
Architect.	Laddie, laddie, it applies up here as well, you know, do you think you're in a different country?
George	*sotto* You can't bloody well win!

CHAPTER 3

A GOOD DAY

Once more it is a Monday morning, and Sir Triard with Lady Sylvia are in their upmarket kitchen.

Sylvia.   You haven't forgotten you're taking all our umbrellas for repair, have you dear?

Triard.   Oh no, of course not.

Sylvia.   Have you found somewhere suitable?

Triard.   Yes, of course; there is an interesting pedestrian way off Southampton Row with cafés and a number of specialist shops - numismatist, umbrellas and so on.

He leaves the room and returns waving four umbrellas.

Sylvia.   Good bye then, have a good day.

He blows a kiss and goes straight to his office where he starts making notes. Miss Firesmoke enters.

Triard.   Ah. Good morning Firesmoke.

Firesmoke.   Good morning, Sir Triard, I hope you had a good weekend.

Triard.   What? Yes of course. Anyhow, Miss Firesmoke, there's a chap starting in the design office today, whom you won't have met, although from your admirable administration you have doubtless met his name.

Firesmoke. Do you mean Mr Brian Sheet, sir?

George Plate enters.

Triard. Ah. Come in, George; I was just mentioning the new man in the design office, Brian Sheet. He's not new to the firm but was recruited overseas some years ago. I see that his personal file is quite thin - a good sign, eh? Firesmoke please introduce yourself to him and let him know what's what and see that he has what he is supposed to have and show him round the office.

Firesmoke. Of course, Sir Triard. - *and leaves* -.

Triard. Now, George, I want you to keep an eye on him. I have given him the Westshire RDC's (Rural Disrtrict Council) works under the Rural Water Supplies and Drainage Act to look after. Take a look at this copy of the Council's letter for him to look at. There seem to be some local complaints of sewage smells in Monk Road and there's the monthly New Works Committee meeting on Wednesday afternoon which someone normally goes to, recently Vernon Mason. I think that Sheet should go to it, having looked at Monk Street in the morning. O.K?

George. Yes, sir, but what about Vernon? He has been looking after Westshire for some time.

Triard.   Oh Yes. Well he is going out to replace Sheet who has done his two years abroad. Before he goes, it would be as well if he took Sheet to Westshire and introduced him to the RE, and perhaps, also start someone off at the reservoir site to help Noble, the RE.

George.   Good, but who?

Triard.   Doesn't really matter; I'll be looking after the project from HQ aspects. Noble is pretty experienced and can handle most things. Go round the office and drag someone from one of the other senior engineers. We're getting a bit overwhelmed all of a sudden. Now for you; what are your plans?

George.   I ought to go to Scotland to sort out the distillery water supply now that the test results have come in.

Triard.   Any problem?

George.   I'm not sure, but they show an unacceptable amount of B.Coli in the existing source.

Triard.   Hm. Well I'm sure you'll be able to deal with that. However, there are two things to do at the Triloughs Hydro scheme. First see that young Jim Culvert is settling in alright. He wanted some site experience and they certainly need help up there. Also, arrange to meet Janet Dropshot and install her as an Assistant RE to William Bridgeman, the

	Engineer's Representative. She knows all about it. You've not been there yet. Its about time she got into something bigger than rural sewerage work and its about time you took on something like the Hydro Scheme as my eyes and ears, especially as you seem to be getting as-it-were up homers in Scotland.
George.	Fine, and thank you very much sir, but 'up homers'?
Triard.	Oh! It's an old Naval expression for a friendly face in a foreign port. Anyhow, things are hotting up. The tunnel work is going great guns, 24 hours a day in three shifts and only half an hour before the morning shift for us to check alignments safely.
George.	How does that fit in with her friend in the Firth Regional Council?
Triard.	If he's not fed up with her quoting Shakespeare, youth will probably find a way.
George.	Right, sir; if it's alright with you I'll go up by the Wednesday night sleeper and come back on Friday night or, perhaps, take in the Burrell museum on Saturday.
Triard.	It's alright for some - off you go.

George goes off. He goes directly to the design office where Brian Sheet and Reg. are working.

George.	Hello. You're Brian Sheet I suppose? I'm George Plate. Where the hell is everyone?
Brian.	Hi. Yes. You may well ask. I gather Ahmed is on day release studying for his HND. The firm seems to have offered to pay his fees if he passes - good idea - anyhow he seems dead keen. Culvert went up to the hydro scheme on Friday, and work has just got the go-ahead on the Molehill Reservoir. And all I've got is young Reg here.
George.	You don't know your luck. I've got to find someone with some site experience to get up there straight away. But how come the office side of the job has come to you? Triard is taking a personal interest.
Brian.	Yes, I know, but I suppose it is because of my dam's experience on the East Bank.
George.	And now you've got the Monk Street smell as well; look at this letter.
Brian.	But I've not got much experience as a water and sewer man.
George.	That's alright. You were on canals weren't you? Well pipes are just closed canals. Water in them flows down hill until its stopped - or pumped. The scheme has been looked after by a capable RE called Sid Blander. He'll show you round and bring you up to date, but it would be as well if you mugged up the contract drawings and hydraulic

calcs before you go; they're in that drawer over there and that box file.

Brian. But how am I going to cope without any help?

George. We all seem to be in the same boat at the moment, but I'll have a word with the partners to see if we can't get you a couple of qualified engineers to help for a time.

Brian. Thank you **very** much, Gerry.

George. No, I'm George; sorry. Not tuned in to the good life yet. Anyhow, you'd better get to Westshire by tomorrow night, meet Sid, and go to the New Works Committee meeting on Wednesday afternoon. They are not a bad lot, and not too political, if you know what I mean. - *Doodoo enters* - Well timed Doodoo. You've met Brian?

Doodoo. Yes. Just because he's short of staff he expects more biscuits. - *She distributes tea and biscuits* -.

George. He needs them, and so do I! The whole office seems to be emptying with all these overseas jobs gelling at the same time. Now, Doodoo, I'm interviewing a candidate in a moment, in Room 14, could you keep an eye open and offer tea to him and another in due course? Please. No, not for me; you've already given me mine.

Doodoo. Okey Doke. I suppose one of my brew is quite enough for you - huh!

George. Don't be like that. We couldn't do without you. *Exit Doodoo. He finishes his tea while pointing things out on the drawings* Look, Brian, let me know if you have any questions.

Brian. What goes on here? Parsimonious with the biscuits, and I just sent down for some staples, and you know what, Miss Firesmoke sent up one strip. And I've been handling a budget abroad of nearly half a million every half year.

George. Yes, she's obviously on the war path. It happens every now and then, probably when a partner observes that the cash flow is a bit tight - nil desperandum - I'm off to Scotland, see you next week, but I'll look in tonight if the interviews don't go on too long.

He leaves in a hurry and goes straight to Room 14, which is set up for interviews. He starts reading a thin file on the desk. There is a knock.

George. Come in. Ah. Good afternoon Miss Firesmoke, I see you've brought in a candidate - *he stands up* - and his wife -er- I presume.

Firesmoke. Yes, Mr Plate, this is Mr John Dicker and Mrs Sheila Dicker. - h*ands are shaken, George indicates a couple of chairs and sits down, not behind the desk. John Dicker is a burly mid thirty ginger bearded healthy looking man. His wife is thin short and mousy in a nice looking way* - I've given them the usual general information and a claim form for

	expenses. Mr Dicker, when you have filled it in, mind you with receipts in support, leave it in my room before you go, and I'll pass it later to Mr Plate for approval.
George.	Yes Miss Firesmoke, that's fine, but there's no need to be too fearsome, we don't want to frighten candidates off.
Firesmoke.	Huh!
George.	Now please notice I've just been on an interview management course and you'll see that I am not sitting behind the desk in an imposing attempt to frighten you. However, it is very inconvenient for writing notes, so if you'll forgive me I'll get behind the desk. I hope that you weren't put off by Miss Firesmoke. If you join us, you won't have much to do with her except that she makes travel arrangements and arranges for payment of salary and expenses.
Dicker.	That's alright, but she is a bit frightening.
George.	Well don't worry. Every cave must have its dragon. If you get the job she'll brief you in detail, and as long as you politely and carefully follow the rules there will be no flames. Now, Mr Dicker, I've read your application and CV which is fine be me so far as technical qualifications go, but you do not appear to have worked overseas?
Dicker.	No sir, I haven't but I've been on short holidays to France and Spain.

George. Good, but you must appreciate that this posting is rather different. You would be living in an LDC - lesser developed country - in a semi arid zone of desert scrub with the occasional sand storm and for three or four months some heavy rain on and off, but otherwise very hot for the rest of the year. You'll be living in temporary accommodation to start with, probably a straw hut to local standards, which aren't too bad, until the contractor, who is on site, has built permanent housing and infrastructure. Any questions, so far?

Dicker. Well sir, what about water supply, power and food and what about medical facilities in an emergency?

George. Good question. The nearest town with useful shops is about 200 miles away where our local HQ is and Project Manager lives. He has the use of a plane and routinely visits the site about once a week. Contact is made in emergency by using the contractor's radio. The contractor will provide electricity, up to 30 amps at 220 volts in the first place, and a small elevated water tank which he will keep topped up. It's groundwater from a borehole in the riverain gravels next to the seasonal river. It's good quality and seems reliable all the year round. Orders for food can be placed with the Project Manager who will get it together for the contractor's weekly overland trip. OK?

Dicker. How long is this likely to go on for and what about storage of perishables?

George. As I say, it depends on the contractor's progress which depends on the country's import regulations etc, but I would be surprised if it was for more than 6 months. Now, we would normally select candidates who have some experience of harsh conditions and different cultures, but they are few and far between these days and your CV is OK otherwise. How can you convince me that you'll be OK? I may say that there'll be at least two couples, probably three, by the time you've served out your notice and got out there.

Dicker. Well, of course, the nearest I've got to such conditions is TV documentaries and travel films, but before we married last year I've spent a good deal of time climbing mountains in Scotland and Wales, sleeping rough on them and you'll see from the CV that I've got the Duke of Edinburgh Award and been on an outward bound course.

George. Were you intending to take your wife with you?

Dicker. Oh yes, of course.

George. Mrs Dicker, how do you feel about that? What sort of travel experience have you had?

Mrs Dicker. Nothing really. I've spent all my life in Bradford, except for an odd trip to Leeds and a walk up Dovedale, but I've a lot of domestic experience. I've been a cook and a hairdresser and kept house for my mother before we got married. If John can manage it, I'm sure I can.

George.   Any more questions? No. OK that seems to wrap it up for now. I'll let you know by the end of the week with an offer or not as the case may be and thank you for coming all this way. Please see Miss Firesmoke on your way out and ask her to bring the next candidate up. Make sure you fill in an expense form.

He ushers them out, makes notes and settles to another file. After all the interviews are over, he has his lunch at The Buckingham in Buckingham Palace Road, two shillings and sixpence for three courses and a half pint of beer. He chats for a while with his favourite taxi driver who is complaining of clutch foot, returns to the office late and goes to Triard's room, where they discuss the candidates.

George.   I come now to the most difficult one, Mr Dicker, who seems OK, well balanced and, at least, has suffered temporary hardships on Scottish mountains, but ..

Triard.   George, don't denigrate that - they can be quite tough - but what?

George.   He wants to take his wife who is a pale shrimp of a thing with apparently no experience of travel beyond getting to Leeds from Bradford. I've got serious doubts about her ability to withstand the culture shock.

Triard.   Hm. Let me think. - *thinks* - Look, George, we're employing the man if you think he's good enough. It's really not our duty to take her into consideration. It's up to them to decide, and she could always come back if it's too much for her. We must make sure she is watched over and get our Project Manager to take special notice until she's settled down.

George. Right, sir, I think it's worth the risk - academically and technically he's better than average. I'll draft offers for him and for two of the others, and, now I must be on my way.

Triard. And so must I; I've got these damned umbrellas to get overhauled. Good night.

They go their separate ways.

* * * * *

Vernon gets to the RE's hut in Westshire the next afternoon, Tuesday, and introduces Brian Sheet to the RE, Sid Blander, over cups of tea.

Vernon. Sid, I'm afraid I'm going to have to leave this job as I've been posted abroad, and Brian, here, is going to take over. I'll show him round the district and then buzz off, but make sure you both visit the Monk Road smell first thing tomorrow or we'll miss the alleged cause of the complaint - and, Sid, when I've finished showing him round, I'll return him to the Bull where you can join him for lunch before the monthly inspection of works in hand. I really must go, now; I've got to get some jabs and update my passport. Cheers, have fun.

He leaves with Brian and drives him round the various villages where work is in hand or planned. Early next morning, Sid drives Brian through the countryside toward Monk Road.

Brian.   Gods! What's that awful smell? - *the car stops -*.

Sid.   That field over there is full of rotting cabbages.

Brian.   And they complain of a bit of fresh sewage smell? This is even worse than the untreated discharge lagoon in the scrub north of Khartoum.

The car starts. They stop at the village centre early on a fine morning; surrounding houses have windows open, but no one is about. Sid and Brian examine a perfectly ordinary manhole cover.

Brian.   Fresh as a daisy.

Sid.   This is the top end of the village sewer system and is where the pumping main from the next village discharges. I think the sewage must stand in the main overnight before the pump cuts in with the morning flushes.

Brian.   Couldn't we just put in a sealed cover here?

Sid.   Not without venting it. Being the top end it could trap explosive gas. We don't want some spark or other to set it off - a lighted cigarette stub thrown in when inspecting the next manhole or something.

Brian. Quite right. I remember my first job when the boss was inspecting a sewer on a perfectly straight road after commissioning. We took the top cover off, and the general started to light his pipe. There was a sheet of flame and all the covers popped up one after the other. Goodness knows what happened to the pipe joints!

Sid. Well the pump has just cut in.

Brian. Yes, there is a bit of a whiff, but really not strong like those cabbages. As Ian Wallace sings "there's something in a sewer which has a strange allure". Now where do you suggest we put a vent column?

They look around pointing to wind vanes, pavements etc. After lunch at a local pub, Sid drops Brian off at the council offices of Westshire RDC. He is taken to a Committee room where the New Works Committee is in session, five men and one woman.

Chairman. Good, that's finished. Now we come to the last item, the Monk's Road smell. Are there still complaints, Estelle?

Estelle. *a bit of a blue stocking with a social conscience* Yes, Chairman, there are. During the last week I have spoken to all the shopkeepers and residents at the top end of the village, and they all confirm that they have been affected, especially on humid windless days.

Chairman. As may be expected. Let's call the consulting

engineer in. This month it is a Mr Brian Sheet who is replacing Vernon Mason whom we have come to know over the past year or two. I propose to send a letter of appreciation to the partners; do you agree? Good, Mr Clerk can you please call him in? - t*he Council's Clerk leaves and re-enters with Brian* - Welcome, Mr Sheet, to this meeting of the New Works Committee and I'm sorry that your first visit involves a complaint; it's about the smell in Monk's Road, Little Stonewall. Mrs Estelle Humphrey-Jones is the councillor for that ward and has confirmed that the problem persists as referred to in my letter last month to Sir Triard. Have you anything to say?

Brian. Thank you, Chairman. May I say it is much appreciated that you invite a representative of the firm to your deliberations and how pleasant it is to meet the members of your committee which we try to serve?

Chairman. Yes, yes, Mr Sheet, but what about the smell?

Brian. Well, sir, at about 8 this morning I was taken to Monk Street by your resident engineer and on the way we passed a field of rotting cabbages which with wind in the right, or should I say wrong, direction would, at least to a townsman like myself, be much more intolerable than a passing smell for a few minutes from the sewer.

Estelle. Two wrongs do not make a right, Mr Chairman, and whereas rotting cabbages from time to time are a burden we have to bear every now and then, we do not expect a new sewage scheme to offend us more or less on a daily basis when we wake up and do our toilet. Windows have to be kept shut, you realize.

Chairman. Yes, I quite agree, so, Mr Sheet, what do you have to say?

Brian. As you know, sir, I am new to the area, but after discussion with the resident engineer it seems likely that the smell emanates from the top manhole in the mornings, as the councillor says, and I did experience a slight smell this morning. It seemed to occur when the pumping main from High Stonewall discharges into it. It seems likely that this would have been the first occasion for some hours overnight, and it is likely that the sewage had as-it-were got over-ripe, slightly septic to be technical, during that period of rest.

Chairman. Sounds plausible, but it still smells.

Brian. What I suggest is that we replace the manhole cover with an air-tight one and vent the manhole, for safety, using a vent column which I suggest could be sited here - *he produces a plan and indicates the spot-*.

Chairman. For safety?

Brian. Yes, because the gas which could accumulate is largely methane, which is very explosive.

Chairman. Good heavens, a smell is bad enough but an explosive one would be intolerable. Carry on, Mr Sheet.

Brian. Quite so. Anyhow this spot is the highest in the village at the junction between the Stonemason Pub and the Post Office. The vent would be about 25 feet high and would finish level with the gutter so as not to spoil any sightlines. There would be an extra cost which I will advise you of as soon as I have had a word with a contractor.

Chairman. Right. Provisionally we all agree, I think.

Estelle. Mr Chairman, I would like the opportunity to approve the appearance, and perhaps Mr Sheet can provide illustrations of alternatives.

Chairman. Yes, of course. Mr Sheet?

Brian. I'll send some options with the quotations. I thought that in the first place we might approach the current contractor for Greenweir's sewerage, being on hand and in the business so-to speak.

Chairman. That's fine and thank you, Mr Sheet, we have no other matters to raise with you today and look forward to hearing from you soon. - *he looks round* - I think that concludes the meeting. Agreed? Good.

They all get up and follow the Clerk and Brian out.

* * * * *

Meantime, George is in Scotland, and has gone to the Glen Dirk distillery, where he is shown to the Manager's office.

George. Well, hello again Mr McStiller.

McStiller. Good morning, Mr Plate. I hope that your journey to these northern territories was pleasant and uneventful, that it will continue to be pleasant and rewarding as this rugged land and its products can make it and that you are both well and able to further our little problem to a verry satisfactory conclusion, towards which we have done our part.

George. Thank you very much for your eloquent welcome, which is much appreciated. And I am looking forward to your account of your findings, but I thought it would be better to start off with the results which we got from the Public Analyst. You will recall that we took samples from the three springs and from the collection/distribution chamber near the factory?

McStiller. Nothing which we would not want to hear, I hope.

George. It all depends. Briefly, all samples are reported to contain more than 10,000 bacteria per 100 millilitres, mostly of B.Coli, and represent water quite unfit to drink without treatment. Is that a problem?

McStiller.   Och. No. All the water that goes to the mash is boiled and what doesn't is used for washing down the floors etc.

George.   The casks and bottles?

McStiller.   All the casks, whether new or repaired, come from our cooperage, - you are acquainted with the word? - outwith the factory, and the bottling is done at a bottling factory near the cooperage.

George.   I like the word 'outwith'. It reminds me of the hymn 'there is a green hill far away without a city wall'. As a child I could never understand why a hill should have had a city wall in the first place. Now if they had used 'outwith' instead all would have been clear. Enough of that. So what did you find was the reason why your forebear forbad the use of the central spring?

McStiller.   We made a great search of the archives and of the diaries of Mr McTavish, who was a most careful and scrupulous manager and, at length, we found that he ordered the discontinued use of the spring because the tied cottagers, or rather their womenfolk, complained that the more peaty browny nature of the water stained their linen when they did the washing.

George.   Good, then that's alright - er - presumably they're on mains water now.

McStiller.   Och no. As I told you last time, they still take it

	from the collecting tank. There's a separate pipe that leads to them.
George.	What! Sorry, I had forgotten. And no complaints of illness?
McStiller.	No no, not that I've heard of. Perhaps it's the whisky which keeps it safe.
George.	Well I'm not sure that you should rely on that. Perhaps, they have developed some sort of natural immunity, but their visitors are unlikely to have the same immunity. But what about the domestic water in the factory, washrooms and drinking water – you know?
McStiller.	Ay. There are special taps for drinking water which is all filtered because we had complaints of rusty water; but, of course, it wasn't rusty; it was its natural colour as in the washroom taps.
George.	Look, Mr McStiller, while I'm here I'd better look at the filtration system and take samples for testing. Better safe than sorry you know. Not all your workers may have developed the immunity your tied cottagers seem to have. I'm seeing the Managing Director the day after tomorrow and will report all this.
McStiller.	Yes, that would be good because I would need her directions before I did anything. Now on the way to the filter room we can go through the still room. You may like to see it, especially as we are

installing a new still. The old one had started to leak, and we don't want to risk any repairs coming into contact with the whisky, you ken?

They walk to the still room. Three beautiful shining copper stills are in place and another ready to install but being hammered in one part with a large mallet.

George. Very impressive, Mr McStiller, but why are they bashing the new still?

McStiller. Och. The old one had a big dent in the same place and we thought that we had better see that the new one is identical - we don't want to risk changing the taste of the whisky, you ken?

* * * * *

It is Friday morning after breakfast with Lady Sylvia in their kitchen.

Sylvia. Now, dear, don't forget it's Friday.

Triard. Thank goodness, but what of it?

Sylvia. You've got to do something today.

Triard. Come on, don't be irritating, Sylvia. I have had a bad week.

Sylvia. Sorry dear, but today's the day you have to collect the umbrellas.

Triard. Yes, yes, of course; don't keep telling me what to do.

Sylvia. Now, now. I think you've been overdoing things. How about seeing our GP for a check up, blood pressure and all that? Shall I fix an appointment for you?

Triard. Oh. Alright, but not on Monday and make sure he doesn't try that new counselling fashion on me. Is that the time? I must rush or I'll miss the train.

He walks to the station and catches his usual train entering the usual compartment and tries to read a journal for the twenty minutes it takes to get to Victoria station when he gets up, reaches into the overhead rack and takes down an umbrella.

Passenger. Hey! That's mine.

Triard. Oh Yes. Sorry; habit I suppose. I do apologise, I don't seem to be myself these days.

Passenger. No problem. Could happen to anyone.

* * * * *

George leaves the distillery and picks Janet up from the Regional Council's offices and proceeds to the Triloughs Hydro Scheme. A tunnel adit is nearby, with a narrow gauge railway coming from it. George and Janet walk up to where William Bridgeman stands outside his office. He is the Engineer's Representative (ER) and an imposing figure, ex Colonel of Royal Engineers type.

George. Well met, sir, how are things going?

Bridgeman. Generally OK, George. The tunnelling is going ahead very quickly if a bit wobbly on line. The shift work system doesn't give us very much time for instrument checks. The main thing, George, is that I'm a bit short of staff. Your new man, Culvert, will be alright I think, but he's got no site experience or know-how at all, and with work opening up on other fronts I do need at least one more useful assistant.

George. Understood, William, that's one of the reasons I've come up here. Shall we go in?

Bridgeman. No, hang on a minute; I'm expecting the Agent who wants a word with you. - *A lorry full of gravel aggregate goes by -.*

George. Let me introduce Janet Dropshot. I thought that she could be one of your section engineers. She's had plenty of site experience. - *Bridgeman and Janet shake hands -.*

Bridgeman. Hm. Girl eh? It can be a bit rough here, you know.

Janet. I grant I am a woman, but I think I can hold my own.

George. Yes, she's no slouch at squash, anyhow, but this will be her first experience of tunnelling.

Bridgeman. She is not bred so dull but she can learn.

George. Sir, sir, she doesn't need prompting. Janet, cool it.

Bridgeman. No matter. Now here comes the Agent and his resident QS, whom I can't stand.

Janet. Why, if it isn't my old oppo, Mr Plank, and if it's not Mr Harry Smart.

A lorry full of aggregate goes by. Harry Smart enters. He is now the Agent.

George. Haven't I seen that one before?

Flash. May be. We have a contract with that firm for a regular supply of aggregate.

They all shake hands etc. and are turning to go into the office, when Jim Culvert comes tearing out of the tunnel as white as a sheet and approaches the ER.

Bridgeman. What on earth's the matter?

Culvert. Sir, there's someone been drowned in the last concrete pour.

Bridgeman. Janet, please go along with him and see what's happened, while we go into the office; you report to me there.

Janet and Culvert leave at a fast trot. They go along the tunnel to where the last concrete pour had been placed. There is shuttering to the height of the springing full of concrete with the soles of a pair of knee boots sticking out.

Janet. Oh. Jim. You've been set up - *taking the*

foreshortened boots off –

Culvert. The bastard!!

Janet. Who?

Culvert. Stanley, our tunnel Section Engineer; he asked me to check that the shuttering hadn't moved before the next shift starts.

Janet. OK. Calm down. It's an old trick, but I'm joining the ER's staff and we'll get our own back in due course. Let's go back now. You go to the canteen for a cuppa and I'll let the ER know what has happened.

Culvert. I'll look an awful fool.

Janet. Don't worry; you're not the first, and Bridgeman seems a sympathetic sort of chap. He won't be pleased, I think.

Meantime, in Bridgeman's office; the party is settled down round a table for meetings at one end. The office is rather bigger and better than most site offices with progress charts and diagrams and the like on those walls where there are no filing cabinets.,

George. Mr Smart, Janet Dropshot is joining our site staff here as a senior Section Engineer. She can manage the attention of the workmen, but I don't want to hear of aggro from your site staff. Understood?

Flash. Yes, of course; we also have a female engineer on our staff, rather younger, but I am sure she'll wise Janet up to who's who and what to watch out for. Changing times!
Anyhow, Mr Plate, the purpose of this preliminary meeting is to advise you and the ER that we are about to make a substantial claim for the cost of excessive overbreak in the soft rock sections of the tunnel. Mr Plank, here, is working it up and will present his workings to Mr Bridgeman next week.

Bridgeman. I wondered what he was doing from time to time at the tunnel face.

George. Look. There's that lorry again - it's the same one. How far away is the quarry?

Flash. A longer round trip than this one seems to take. I'll look into it.

George. Thank you for the notice of claim. We'll minute it as formally advised. However, neither I nor Mr Bridgeman intend to discuss it now. William, please let me have your comments on it in due course if you can't sort it out up here. If it is pursued and has substance, remember that we, that is head office, have a duty to inform the client of anything substantial.

Bridgeman. Of course. Ah. - *Janet enters* - Janet, come in and tell us what all that was about.

Janet. Someone has pulled an old trick on Culvert, sir, who is a bit young to see the funny side of it. In fact, he's more than a bit upset. - so I sent him off to the canteen to recover.

Bridgeman. What sort of trick?

Janet. A pair of shortened knee boots were stuck upside down on the new concrete. Don't worry; I am sure we'll find a way to deal with it in due course.

Agent. Now, now, I hope it wasn't one of my staff - I'll have his what-knots - if it was.

Janet. No sir; I'll discuss it with Mr Bridgeman first.

Bridgeman. You do that Janet. I don't want trouble. She speaks poniards and every word stabs.

George. Don't worry, Mr Smart. She's always quoting Shakespeare and seems to have set Mr Bridgeman off. At least I think it was Shakespeare. - *there's a hammering on the door, enter a foreman and someone else -*.

Flash. Can't this wait, Eric?

Foreman. I thought you'd want to know straight away. This chap is one of the drivers of the aggregate lorries and has just stopped by my office and given himself up.

Agent. Come on then; what's he done?

Driver. Well, it was too easy. I just couldn't go on doing it. It was like taking tits out of a baby's mouth.

Agent. What was? Though I think I'm beginning to see.

Driver. Well, I comes in with my load and gets the delivery chit signed at the gate, then I puts a tarpaulin over the lot and drives out the other end of the site and gets a chit signed for spoil to the tip. Then I stops for a smoke and then go round again. I'm sorry, sir, but - w*hat he had to say was drowned in gusts of laughter from everyone except Flash –.*

Flash. I think you had better come with me to my office - now!

* * * * *

The next evening, Friday, George reports to the Office of the MD of Scottish Distilleries Ltd.

George. Well, Mrs McNash, that's about it. I'll send you a written report next week. It seems fairly clear to me, subject to tests on the drinking water; the Glen Kirk distillery can increase its capacity by 50% using the third spring provided that you do something about the supply to the tied cottages. We can help you there if you choose to treat the water locally; but bearing in mind the cost and continuing responsibility of local treatment you may think it best, in the first place, to approach the water company.

McNash.   Thank you Mr Plate for your investigation and I look forward to your written report for me to put before the Board with my recommendations, which I am sure will follow your advice. - Now, George it looks as though it's after five thirty on a Friday night. I think we may reasonably have a dram, don't you?

George.   Thank you very much, Clare, that will go down very well. I wonder whether you'll come out with me for dinner tonight. Sorry about the short notice.

McNash.   I'd like to very much but I have another do to attend. Perhaps another time. Are you going back tonight?

George.   Yes, but I'm hoping to bring my wife up the next time I visit, in particular to see the Burrell collection. I hear it's worth a visit.

McNash.   Yes it is, and you may find the building itself interesting, too. I know; would you let me take you both to it and show you round? It's some time since I went there myself.

George.   That would be splendid. I'll consult her and you for a convenient date. Now, what do you think of post-modern art - and, before you answer, this really is a very good drop, I….

* * * * *

In London at much the same time, a train draws into a suburban station. Triard reaches into the over-head rack and takes out four umbrellas.

Passenger.   I see you have had a good day today! Picked up quite a few, haven't you?

Triard   *tired and in high dudgeon* I'll thank you sir, but they are all mine. A good day, indeed!

CHAPTER 4

A BIG SMELL

Sir Triard is about to leave his wife for work on a Monday morning.

Sylvia.   Now, Triard, remember you've been ill.

Triard.   Yes, yes, of course.

Sylvia.   So, yes, yes, of course what?

Triard.   Of course, I'll take things easy and try not to get upset and I'll remember to take my pill at lunch-time.

Sylvia.   Excellent. Where is it? - *Triard goes through his pockets* - It's in a little sachet attached to your watch in your watch pocket, so when you consult it near lunch-time to see if the office clock is right it will come to mind.

Triard.   Very clever, Sylvia. Now I really must go or I shall be off to a bad start.

They exchange kisses and he leaves for his office where he sends for George.

Triard.   Well, George, had a good weekend?

George.   Yes, thanks - mostly digging up weeds from the lawn and replacing them with grass dug from the flower beds. How about, you? Are you fully recovered and like a greyhound on the slips straining at the start as Janet would say?

Triard. Now George, stop that; one in the firm is quite enough and not so much of the grey either. Now, I don't know what your plans are, but there's one thing you really have to sort out and that's the Monk Road smell at Westshire. See Sheet's memo of the last meeting with the New Works Committee. It's the sort of piddling little thing that can get seriously out of hand. We don't want to upset them – they've been very good clients, ever since your father did the first job for them before the war.

George. I didn't know that. Anyhow, I'll try to sort out the smell to everyone's satisfaction. Brian Sheet has doubtless got his head well into it sniffing out the problem.

Triard. Well, and while you are about it could you take a preliminary look at their Square Grove sewage works. The council have had complaints from the River Purification Board about the effluent quality. The existing works was one of our first jobs for Westshire - You may find something about them in the archives store in the basement. Now what else is there? – Remember, my wife has told me take it easy.

George. If you agree, I would like to visit the Triloughs Hydro Scheme to see how Janet is settling in and

	for a preliminary look at the overbreak claim. We had a formal notice of it from the contractor while you were away.
Triard.	Ah. Yes. It looks as though it could be substantial, although at present it seems to be more in the realms of a Clause 52 valuation, rather than a dispute. It needs clarification at least. Now let me see; Euan Fairview left a phone message to say that he would welcome some advice relating to a claim relating to some amendment in a letter of acceptance. You might look in on him and our Scottish office as a bit of a morale booster. Also, to take his mind off the smell which he has run into, could you get Brian Sheet to call in on the new reservoir site to see how the new ARE is getting on and whether the RE, Robert Noble, know him? is happy.
George.	Good. No, I don't know Mr Noble. Well, I'll get on with it, but I think Euan's query may have to wait until next visit if it can't be dealt with in correspondence.
Triard.	Oh. Hang on a minute. I've just remembered a panic cry from Euan which could be a problem and certainly needs some Head Office back-up. It's about the foundations on old coal workings for some high rise blocks of flats. According to Euan the building contractor is unhappy with our work, and his design consultant is creating an idea that we were not up to the job. Small local firm and local contractor possibly trying to make

capital out of it. You had better see to that.

George. OK. I'll try to fit that in this week and may be able to deal with Euan's other problem at the same time.

Triard. Yes, do, otherwise I can see claims for delay being laid at our door. Now off you go.

George proceeds at once to Miss Firesmoke's office. A wooden slide on the door says that she is in, and he knocks.

Firesmoke. Come in.

George. Ah! Miss Firesmoke, how are things going?

Firesmoke. As well as can be expected, Mr Plate, but we do our best, don't we?

George. I'm sure you do. It's probably not necessary to say so, but I don't think Sir Triard is back to full strength yet and I am sure you'll do your best to see that he doesn't get bothered with trivial matters.

Firesmoke. Oh. I do so agree. I'll have a word with his secretary to consult me on any disagreeable matter, and if it's not likely to create, I'll try to get Mr Highway to deal with it. Would you have a word with him, please?

George. Right, I will; that seems OK for the time being. Now, I'm off to Scotland again - so could you get

	me an overnight sleeper for tomorrow night with a stop-over at Perth and return on Sunday night. I'm trying to get my wife to join me on Friday for a long weekend - she'll be all the better for it.
Firesmoke.	Certainly, Mr Plate, my pleasure. Shall I book your wife's ticket too?
George.	Yes please, and fix times with her direct, if you can, and thanks, Miss Firesmoke. What a treasure! - *he leaves*
Firesmoke	*to herself.* Creep. Nice long notice he gives. What are they going to do with the baby, I wonder? As long as he doesn't want me to look after it!

Meanwhile, in the design office, which is full and busy. Brian is on the telephone.

Brian. Is that Mrs Workington? - good, my name is Brian Sheet. - No, SHEET as in bed! - Yes, that's it. I'm from Noplay & Partners - we are the consulting engineers for the council looking after the sewerage - yes, the drains in your district - no, I keep telling you the name's SHEET. - what? - Well, all the main sewers, drains, have been laid and we are now arranging house connections to them, which probably seems about time, too. - Yes, I agree, but your house is rather a special case because your two neighbours cannot be connected directly - well not without going through your garden, and you wouldn't want that would you? ……….So we want to lay a connection pipe up your back passage …. ….No please don't take it like that - in more exact terms in your access drive and footpath at the back of your garden, which forms a right of way for your neighbours .. -… OK, back passage is a quicker way of saying it - yes, and my name is still SHEET - *he goes on talking as George enters -*.

George. Well, good to see a full office and you all working away. Ahmed, who are these two?

Ahmed. This is John Jewel and that is Jack Paul.

George. Hi. John, I wanted to see you to arrange a visit for Brian to introduce you to the RE at the reservoir site. Should be good experience.

John. Fine, the sooner the better; the happier I'll be on site.

George. Where do you live?

John. Near Potters bar. - *Sheet puts down the phone, blows his nose, and starts hovering near George -*.

George. Excellent. Brian can pick you up at Potters Bar station, say, and take you on in my car at, say, 9.30. Brian, it's a red Ford Zephyr. Here are the keys; it's parked in Greycoat Lane. Take care with it and don't think you're Sterling Moss. If it's not raining, you can have the hood down - easier to spot. John, bring boots, duffel coat and so on. - *John nods, but Brian still hovers* - Ahmed, salaam, how are you getting on with your day release course?

Ahmed. Quite well, I think, thanks. I have had a bit of trouble getting the hang of strain energy, but Ed has helped me with a bit of tuition.

George. That could be tricky. He knows his stuff but is not the best communicator in the world. That sounds like him now.

Ed. *outside, shouting* But it's all to do with Froude numbers and exit velocity.

Hydrologist *outside, shouting back* Yes, of course, but have you decided on the nature of the cut-off?

Ed. Well, if we want to recover as much head as possible.

Hydrologist. But what's that got to do with the cut-off?

Ed. Well, it's a question of downstream scour protection. You see what I mean?

Hydrologist. No. Do <u>you</u> see what <u>you</u> mean? - *George shuts the door* -.

George. You see what I mean, Ahmed. Yes, Brian, what's the problem?

Brian. The Monk Road smell. I could do with some help. You know I recommended sealing the top manhole and putting in a vent column. I'm going to the New Works Committee meeting on Wednesday to tell them its in place but not connected. Frankly. I'm scared that it may not work in all conditions.

George. Agreed. From what I hear we ought to look more carefully at the design, and if there's a design fault try to correct it when the vent column is connected. Then all faces will be saved.

Brian. Our noses will not be out of joint.

George. Quite, as-it-were keeping them clean. Now, where are the contract drawings? - - ---- *Brian gets them out and they start studying them. George looks up* - Jack, I almost forgot. We've been asked by Westshire RDC to look at their Square Grove sewage treatment works. It's an old one, pre-war. Sir Triard says that there should be some data on it in the basement archives; somewhere in the mid thirties, I gather. Do you think you could try to find it and bring it up here? - *Jack leaves* - Now, Brian, it looks as though the design is to have a gravity sewer draining along this higher ground to the main sewage treatment works with pumping mains from three villages discharging into it well away from the buildings; so how come there is any smell at all?

Brian. According to the RE, Sid, our Mr Teak looked after the job in the early stages and thought that cost could be saved by routing the pumping main from Little Shoreham to Monk Road for onward pumping to a much shorter sewer. So he issued a variation order; here it is.

George. But the pumping main from Little Shoreham rises before it falls to Monk Road, i.e. to where the gravity sewer was to start, and he's put an air valve at the top. It may be good practice for a water main, but it does mean that all this down hill stretch empties when the pumping stops. What do you say to that?

Sheet. Foul air can accumulate overnight.

George. Looks a distinct possibility. I wonder if Teak took into account the present value of the cost of double pumping. I doubt it, but the missing sewer can always be put in later if the flows get too big. Anyhow, good luck with the meeting. - *Jack returns with some box files* - No rest. Thanks, Jack. Where's Doodoo - let's have a look at these. Good heavens it's in my father's handwriting - And here's a closing letter to the District Clerk sending finished drawings. Let me have a look at this…

* * * * *

Mr and Mrs Brian Sheet are at home on their entrance drive. It is an unsurfaced hoggin, or all-in gravel, drive with raised concrete kerbs each side. He is on his motor-bike.

Brian. Well, Sweet, today's the day the concrete comes.

Frances. Yes, I know. Anything else I ought to know?

Brian. I've asked for it to come in a ready-mix transit mixer. You know, those big round things that hold

	up the traffic. Well, it's got some distance to come so I specified that water is added at site.
Frances.	Where's that?
Brian.	Now, now, if I had time I'd show you. - *he revs his bike* - So they'll add the water here, and I don't want the concrete to be too wet.
Frances.	What can I do about that?
Brian.	Not much, in fact, but you can try. I've specified no more than a two and a half inch slump. It's measured by tamping a sample into a steel cone and taking the cone off to see how far it slumps.
Frances.	You don't expect me to do that in front of all the men?
Brian.	No, of course not, but I suggest you ask the driver before he adds water whether he's got a slump cone on board.
Frances.	OK. Could be interesting. I'll have to think what to wear.
Brian.	Hm! Anyhow, before I go to Westshire RDC tonight, Council meeting tomorrow, I'll be out of the office most of today at a reservoir site; here's the RE's telephone number, a Mr Noble. God's, I'll miss the train. - *they kiss and he roars off down the drive* -

* * * * *

At the reservoir site, the Zephyr draws up by the RE's hut. Noble comes out of the hut as Brian and John Jewel leave the car.

Brian. Good morning, Mr Noble. I'm Brian Sheet and this is John Jewel who is joining you.

Noble. Good. I've been expecting you and needing help for some time. John, I hope you'll live up to your name.

Jewel. Above rubies, sir, I hope.

Noble. Like my wife? Well come inside for a cup of tea; it's ready for you! - *they go inside and come out holding mugs* - Well, the immediate tasks are two level surveys. One on this site here, or rather the part where the dam goes, and the other at the borrow pit where the fill is coming from. - *they look at the site, Noble pointing out things* -

Brian. Thanks for the tea, but if you'll excuse me I'd better be off. - *he leaves with the noise of revving Zephyr in pole position* -

Noble and Jewel. Bye.

Noble. I'll take you to meet the contractor and his staff shortly, especially the one you'll be agreeing the survey with. Are you married?

Jewel.   No.

Noble.   Pity.

Jewel.   Why?

Noble.   Where are you staying?

Jewel.   In a local pub for a night or two while I find somewhere more permanent and cheaper. Any ideas?

Noble.   Possibly, you'd better have a word with the baker tomorrow morning. He knows everything that goes on around these parts.

* * * * *

Back at Brian Sheet's drive. Frances approaches a small lorry where it has parked on the grass alongside a rather rickety looking portable lavatory, and a ganger and two workmen stand with shovels and a tamper at the ready. A transit mixer backs up the drive.

Ganger.   You Mrs Sheet?

Frances.   *in a beekeeper's outfit* Yes. Glad you got here alright. Do you need a tap for the water?

Ganger.   No thanks. We carry it with us.

Frances.   You remember the spec. No more than a two and a half inch slump.

Ganger. *looks at the others with a what have we got here expression* Yes, miss; We'll see to it - no sloppy mix.

Frances. That's the way. Have you got a slump cone on board?

Ganger. Of course; want to see it? - *he produces it -*

Frances. Good. I'll get back to my hives. Let me know when you're ready for a tea-break.

She goes off to her hives with a wave of the smoking smoker.

* * * * *

George is in his own office. Open box files are on desk and his secretary is seated opposite.

Laura. Laura, a letter to the District Clerk, Westshire RDC, heading Square Grove Sewage Works. Dear Mr District Clerk - yes, I know it's an unusual form of address, but it was used by my father, so I thought it would be nice to keep in the tradition - Thank you very much for your letter dated 29 May 1957 inviting us to make a preliminary report on what the Council might do to prevent further complaints from the River Purification Board. Para - We refer to our letter Dated 4th June 1934 - yes, Laura thirty four - in which we sent as-built drawings for the sewage works and a summary of design data. You will note - yes, Laura, new para - that we advised at the time that the Works were designed and the land acquired for eventual doubling of its capacity, should that be needed. Para - Our Mr Brian Sheet will be attending the New Works Committee meeting on Wednesday afternoon next, and we hope that you can spend some time after it to brief him on current population, trends and forecasts and the status of available land near the existing Works. Yours truly Yes, I know, Laura, its not our usual ending, but I think the convention is to use this when you're being friendly but have not yet met the chap. Laura, please get it typed and signed by Sir Triard or another partner if necessary and posted today.

Laura. Yes, sir; at once sir.

George. Alright, alright. Very good, Miss.

* * * * *

There are two cars parked side by side at the edge of the borrow pit, whence gravel is taken (not borrowed) for making the reservoir's dam. Beside the cars are an absolutely stunning girl in well fitting dungarees, a chainman, levelling pegs etc. and John Jewell.

John. Sorry I'm late; you're Doreen? I see what Mr Noble meant; what's the plan?

Doreen. What did Mr Noble say? Perhaps I might guess - no matter - the first thing is to get here on time; we don't want claims for delay floating about, do we?

John. No, Doreen, I'm very sorry, but

Doreen. No buts. OK. Right, Kelvin here has set out all those ranging rods on a grid using temporary stakes in the hedges so that we can always re-establish the grid, and we are going to take ground levels at each point. I suggest that I take the reading first, then you check it, and we record it.

John. Sounds fine, as long as we don't make the same mistake. Hi, Kelvin. Now let me see, I've got my level book, two pencils - Ah! But no rubber.

Kelvin. I've got the rubber. Engineers don't make mistakes!

John. But you'll be miles away when I want it.

Doreen. Then you won't be making mistakes, will you? That concrete post over there will do for our TBM back-sight.- *she sets up the level and Kelvin goes to the Temporary Bench Mark and puts the staff on it. Doreen makes arm signals to get the staff upright –*

John. Oughtn't he to be moving at back and forth a bit so that we can get the lowest reading?

Doreen. Yes, he's fairly new to this sort of work. - *shouts* - Kelvin, get directly behind the staff to keep it upright one way, and move it fore and aft a bit to be sure of passing through the vertical. That's it - *they take readings, confer, agree and write them down. Kelvin moves to the first grid spot. Doreen takes her reading and notes it down. John goes to the instrument and sights over it –*

John. Kelvin, why have you got the staff on your toe? Doreen, he doesn't seem all that new to the job, and is this the sort of trick you play for measuring excavations?

Doreen. No, of course not. Kelvin, what do you think you were doing?

Kelvin. I was told by one of the lads it was the thing to do.

Doreen. Well it isn't and don't ever do it again - besides it can sometimes work against us.

John. Oh. Ho!

Doreen. Oh. Ho. Come on let's get on with it. Kelvin, move.

They continue taking level readings for most of the morning.

* * * * *

Brian Sheet makes good time and is called in to the committee room where Westshire RDC New Works Committee is in session.

Chairman. Welcome Mr Sheet. Good of you to come. Sit down. … Any news on the smell?

Brian. Thank you, Mr Chairman. It fits in very well as

	I am meeting your Clerk afterwards to get some data relevant to Square Grove sewage works. It was very good of you to invite us for a preliminary report.
Chairman.	Yes, yes. Glad to see that you're getting on with it, the River Purification Board is being very insistent. But what about the smell? The ward councillor will be very interested to hear.
Estelle.	Yes, indeed. Last week Mr Sheet forwarded through the RE some designs, one of which I advised was appropriate.
Chairman.	But what about the smell?
Brian.	I can report that the vent column to the approved design has been erected. By the way is the smell still there?
Estelle.	No, Mr Chairman; at least, I've had no complaints.
Brian.	That's funny, the column has not yet been connected.
Chairman.	Now Mr Sheet, that may seem funny to you, but it is not to me. Don't do anything like that again.
Brian.	I apologise. A slip of the tongue I'm afraid I couldn't resist. No. I shall resist any such opportunity in the future. Anyhow, the connection is being made this afternoon, and I hope that

you'll have no reason to raise the matter again, - but in the unlikely event that you do, you will doubtless let me know, and I shall visit immediately and in person to investigate, and if the fault lies with the siting of the vent column the visit will be at no charge.

Chairman. That's what I like to hear, putting you money where your mouth is, or should I say nose? Can you come up to our next month's meeting and give an outline of your findings in respect of the Square Grove works, and be prepared for questions about the smell?

Brian. Yes, sir, I see no reason at present why I can't come, and will be glad to.

Chairman. Good. Now off you go with the District Clerk and as usual this was the last item on the Agenda; any other business? - good. - *all get up and start dispersing* -

* * * * *

Meanwhile, at the start of a busy tour, George enters the Contractor's site office for Kithwheel High Rise Building; He is surprised to find seven men round the table, cramped, and with a distinct air of hostility. After notional greetings:

Agent. Well, Mr Plate, you understand our problem. We are not happy about the foundations, that the mine workings have been properly filled.

George.   Yes. So I'm given to understand.

Agent.   Well the floor is yours.

George.   Thank you. I didn't expect such a large contingent and must thank the contractor for letting me use this office as ours would have been too small. Now, before getting down to the nutty gritty as-it-were, to coin a phrase, can I ask you who you all are? Mr Smart, we have met before, and what are you doing here? Aren't you the agent at the Triloughs Hydro Scheme any more?

Flash.   No. I am still that, but this is one of my earlier responsibilities as contracts manager, and I hope to see the end of them after this.

George.   Thanks. I understand; your post at Triloughs must be demanding enough for one man. Anyhow, perhaps you could do the introductions. Mr Fairway you all know is the manager of our Scottish office and I am the representative from head office with, at present, responsibility to the partners for work in Scotland. Right, Mr Smart, please go ahead.

Flash.   This is my agent for the contract to build these high rise flats on top of the old mine workings which we understand were your responsibility to make safe. This is Mr Callow, our construction adviser who with me and the agent decided to call in a consulting engineer, Mr Kinsey, there, to advise us. And this is the well known and respected mining engineer, Mr Cambourne, brought in by Mr Kinsey as a sort of ultimate authority.

George. Thank you, Mr Smart, and I am very pleased that you all, as interested parties, have made time to visit together. Separate discussions would have been very time taking and possibly indeterminate. Now with so many involved a sort of open forum discussion would be difficult to handle at this stage, but may be worthwhile later on. So as I have the floor or, more accurately, the chair could I ask you to address your remarks to me until I give the go-ahead for a free for all. So, I'm going to start with you Mr Smart; would you lead off?

Flash. I think my agent is better placed.

George. Well, sir, can you start off?

Agent. I think, having engaged a construction adviser, who confirmed our view that the workings might not be safe as foundations - perhaps he should start.

George. Good. Now, Mr Callow, why should you think there's a problem?

Callow. We don't know that there is a problem, but my clients were not involved in the mine filling operation and we thought that we ought to be sure of the foundations before building on them - as a sort of duty of care to both our insurers and the building developer. It seemed best to call on a consulting engineer to advise on the proper procedures. Hence I suggest that Mr Kinsey can take up the story.

George.   Mr Kinsey, it looks as though you have the baton, or is it the buck?

Kinsey.   No, the buck stops with Mr Cambourne, because it seemed to me that the shortest possible route would be for you to convince an independent expert that all is well.

George.   Thank you, but are you not independent?

Kinsey.   Of course, but although I have experience of foundations in general, I cannot be said to have the experience, knowledge or reputation of Mr Cambourne as to mines.

George.   Thank you Mr Kinsey, very handsome of you. Now, Mr Cambourne it looks as though it's down to you and me. Could you perhaps come to the drawing board over there and I can show you what has been done? - *George and Cambourne move to the board where George uncovers a large sheet, while drinks come in and the others relax, light cigarettes and smirk* - Now this is a record showing all the holes drilled by depth and date - and if you want to check, Euan Fairway has the drilling contractor's logs here for you to look at - *pause* - You'll see that we worked through the site progressively with alternate holes drilled and lined in rows through the workings to the bottom and in alternate rows drilled but lined only to the top of the cavities. Where there was no cavity we drilled nearby until we were successful.

Cambourne. Yes, I understand that existing records of practice at the time showed that coal was cut leaving uncut coal as supports instead of the props we use nowadays. Ah. I see that the shallow holes are half way between deep holes on each grid line.

George. Yes, that's right. Grouting proceeded in each deep shell until grout appeared at one or other adjacent shallow one, and you can see how the progression worked satisfactorily.

Cambourne. studies and thinks. Yes, that seems alright as far as it goes. But it is circumstantial evidence, good circumstantial evidence, but to be convinced I would need to see some cores. - *turns to the Agent* - Have you seen the cores?

Agent. No, none have been shown to us.

Euan. Fffor Ggggheaven's sake. The iiinformmation in yyyour ttttender dddocuments tttold yyou where they cccould be seen. All this pppalaver is bbbecause yyyou couldn't tttake the tttrouble to lllook.

George. Now calm down Euan; oversights do occur in the panic of tendering. - *turns to the Agent* - Now, why don't you go along to the Council's warehouse

123

where they are and satisfy yourself? Mr Fairway will take you.

Agent. I'd much rather Mr Cambourne went; he knows what to look for. Can you come Mr Cambourne? I know you have another appointment this afternoon, but this matter has been hanging about too long already.

Fairway. *sotto* Fffestering yyyou mean.

Cambourne. If we can go straight away and I miss lunch - probably no bad thing for me - yes, let's go.

* * * * *

Janet Dropshot and an engineer in donkey jacket emblazoned "MacAllwork Section Engineer" stand in the main hall of the generator house, Triloughs Hydro Scheme. One wall is faced with wooden shutters ready to receive concrete. There is much hammering and shouting from inside it.

Janet *sotto* I think you should let him out now.

Engineer. Yes, I think so. He should have learnt his lesson by now.

Janet. But you didn't know anyone was in there.

Engineer. No, of course not. Can't think how he came to be in there.

Janet. But how are you going to proceed?

Engineer. I'll get the concrete foreman to nominate Thickear to give a final inspection of the joint surface inside the shuttering. Even he is bound to reckon something is wrong. Touching, really, as he had been the one to nail up the last sheet.

Janet. Clever.

Engineer. Yes. He's almost completely deaf from working jack hammers all his life, so when Stanley gets out his language is not likely to affect him much.

Later, Thickear is taking down one of the sheets and Stanley bursts out, shouting

Stanley. How much bloody longer were you going to leave me. Oh! Thickear, - *even louder* - what do you know about this?

Thickear. What?

Stanley. Locking me up in there.

Thickear. Er. I don't know nowt. Foreman told me to take down a sheet what I put up a couple of hours ago.

Stanley. Who told the bloody foreman?

Thickear. I dunno.

Stanley. When I find him, I'll make him a timorous beastie and put a right panic in his bloody breastie.

They leave, Stanley fuming and red in the face.

Meantime, a meeting is in session in the ER's office with Harry Smart the Agent, Mr Plank Q.S., Bridgeman the ER, and George Plate. Drawings and photos are on the table.

Plank. So you see, the nature of the rock is that it could not be excavated practically without exceeding the limit of overbreak shown on the drawing, for which measurement is on the superficial area of the tunnel segment's surface.

George. So?

Plank. So the volume of excavated material evidenced by the shift records is much more than we planned for or could reasonably have expected, and worse still the amount of concrete and grout needed to fill the annulus is correspondingly increased.

Bridgeman. George, you will see from the drawings that the limit of overbreak is shown by a dotted line and from the spec that the contractor was not expected to work outwith this line, but only to excavate what was reasonable within it.

Flash. But the nature of the rock was that it was not reasonable to keep within it.

Bridgeman. If that is true, do we get a reduction in the rate for the lengths where you did not use up the allowance?

Plank. Of course not. Our price is for overbreak per square yard and what allowances we made is our business but apart from the extra excavation and concrete there is the effect of consequent delay …. What the - *the door bursts open and in comes a very red faced Stanley followed closely by Janet -*.

Bridgeman. Now, what do you think you're doing breaking in on our meeting, like this?

Stanley. Sir, sorry, but with everyone here my complaint can be heard.

Bridgeman. Later.

Janet. Sir, it appears that the steel fixing and shuttering were complete over the weekend and Stanley insisted on a panel being removed and the Section Engineer said it wasn't necessary and would delay casting a whole day. I gather the row got a bit fierce until a sheet of formwork was removed.

Stanley. He's an obstinate bugger and has it in for me.

Bridgeman. Quiet, both of you, and both leave now, and come to me with the agent and his Section Engineer this afternoon - *he looks at the Agent* OK? *Stanley and Janet nod and leave -*.

Flash. Yes, OK by me but I smell a fish.

Bridgeman. So do I.

George. Why?

Bridgeman. Well there may have been a conspiracy to get back on Stanley for his rather callous treatment of that youngster, Culvert; you heard about that? Anyhow, Mr Plank, sorry about that, please proceed.

Plank. As I was saying, there's the effect of the consequential delay, particularly of constructional plant.

George. But as I understand it, a daily rate for delay on site as a whole has been agreed for constructional plant.

Plank. But there's an individual measurable element due to overbreak.

George. But you can't have it both ways.

Plank. That's not the point. Here we have a known attributable delay, the consequences of which are measurable.

George. Mr Smart, can't you stop this?

Flash. No, I think he has a valid point.

George. Well, I don't think it can be discussed further here with any benefit. Yes, William?

Bridgeman. It may not be necessary to take it further if we can get back to the overbreak itself. You may not know, George, that on this section the contractor broke the UK record for soft rock tunnelling.

George. Good. Congratulations. It is good to hear that the contractor was not causing a delay.

Plank. Humph. Not the same thing as being delayed.

Bridgeman. I hadn't finished. To do this, the gangs were in three shifts on piece work, which made it very difficult for us, and, indeed, the contractor to check direction, but we did take photographs of the working face from time to time and here they are.

Flash. So what?

Bridgeman. So the tunnellers were not careful. You can see evidence of where drill rods were themselves outside the overbreak limit and - *the meeting continues –*.

Much later, in the same office, Bridgeman, Smart, Janet, Stanley and the Section Engineer are all present.

Bridgeman. Now, Mr Smart, shall I lead off or will you?

Flash. No. Go ahead, please.

Bridgeman. Now, look here you three. I don't know what all the rights and wrongs are, but the fact is that we have every right to inspect existing concrete and steel fixing before new concrete is placed. So, in

> this respect, Stanley was correct in his insistence for access.

Engineer. Yes, of course, but not at that time. He knew our programme and he would have been welcome to inspect on Sunday evening.

Flash. You'll remember, Mr Bridgeman, that we got your permission to work this section over the weekend.

Bridgeman. Yes. We may have been short in planning for it. Off you go, Stanley, and you Mackilroy. Janet, you stay behind. Mr Smart, there's obviously a good deal of aggro between those two, and I don't want it to get out of hand whether or not Mackilroy was in on it.

Flash. Agreed. If I may make a suggestion, one or other should be moved to new duties.

Bridgeman. Not one but both, otherwise there will be loss of face, which is not a good thing on a site like this.

Flash. Agreed, again. I can put the section engineer on the construction of the penstocks.

Bridgeman. Janet. Where are we most short?

Janet. On the collection intakes on the upper moors.

Bridgeman. Agreed. I'll fix that and put that youngster, Jim Culvert, to take over at the generation station, but Janet, you'll have to keep a close eye on him. I'll

	brief him to report to you. Well, that seems to be settled, Mr Smart.
Flash.	Yes. Couldn't be better. They couldn't be further apart, and Stanley will be in his element on the moors. Well, I'll be off now. - *he goes -*.
Bridgeman.	Janet, as he must needs thrust his neck into a yoke, he must wear the print of it. When Stanley has writ his daily report I think I'll see Mackilroy and you between the sheets.
Janet.	It is not so nor t'was not so; but, indeed, God forbid it should be so.
Bridgeman.	Quite so, we don't want much ado about nothing. Be careful, Janet.
Janet.	Sir, it was my school play. - *she leaves Bridgeman holding back a smile -*.

* * * * *

Back in London, Sir Triard enters the design office and is furious to find it empty.

Triard.	What the devil? - *Brian Sheet enters* - What's the meaning of this? It's intolerable.
Brian.	Sir, sir, may I explain? - *other staff enter -*.
Triard.	You had better, and where's George Plate? Oh. I remember, he's in Scotland.

Brian. Yes. You see sir, Doodoo, the tea lady, has been off sick and there has been no replacement for most of the week, which we have worked through without as-it-were a tea break, so being Friday afternoon we thought we'd go to the café next door.

Triard. And how long did this take?

Brian. I suppose no more than twenty minutes, sir.

Triard. Far too long. It mustn't happen again. - *he starts to leave -*.

Brian. Sir, please listen a minute.

Triard. Well?

Brian. The bad news is that by some sort of telepathy other design offices had the same idea. The good news is that the conversation was entirely about work and we found it helpful to swap experience with others,

Triard. Telepathy, indeed.

He leaves the room still in high dudgeon and, not feeling well, decides to leave early. On the way to the station he starts to cross the road near a corner. A taxi turns the corner quickly, forcing Sir Triard to jump backwards and the taxi to halt, tyres screaming. Sir Triard bangs the driver's window with his umbrella. The driver winds down his window.

Driver. What's the matter gov.

Triard. I'm not your gov, worst luck, but I've a bad heart and you didn't do it any good.

Driver. But you're alright now, aren't you?

Triard. Yes, but no thanks to you - have you got a horn?

Driver. Course I have.

Triard. Does it work?

Driver. Course it does.

Triard. Well, let's hear it then. - *the driver gives a good blast on it* - That's far too long and far too late.

He strides off, momently full of nervous energy and waving his umbrella.

CHAPTER 5

SING A SONG OF SIXPENCE

Sir Triard enters their kitchen on yet another Monday morning.

Sylvia.   Now, Triard, do you really think you're OK to go back to work?

Triard.   Of course I am. Do you think I'd dress up like this if I weren't?

Sylvia.   Yes. Quite likely. You had an upsetting time at the end of last week what with an empty office and nearly being run down by a taxi. You had hardly relaxed enough to watch 'Yes Minister' last night.

Triard.   I know, but I'm alright now.

Sylvia.   I think you have been doing too much. Can't you get another partner to spread the load? What about George Plate - he seems the right sort?

Triard.   Yes, he probably is partner material, but not quite ready for it yet even though his hair seems to be going prematurely grey. Anyhow he couldn't afford it at the moment.

Sylvia.   How is he ever going to afford it?

Triard.   See your point. I'll discuss it with the other partners. We may come up with something.

Sylvia. Good. Now don't put it off - and have a good day. I don't want to be widowed just yet.

Triard. I'll try to keep alive.

Sylvia. And what are you going to do about the empty office? You can't just leave it and, besides, Brian has a point about lateral discussion.

Triard. Alright. I'll think about it. Perhaps an occasional arrangement could be made.

Sylvia. For goodness sake, don't make it too formal, it would be a real turn-off.

Triard. Where do you get these phrases from? No, I'll discuss it with the other partners when we discuss George's position.

Sylvia. Good. That's better. Positive thinking always puts you in a better mood. Bye love.

Sir Triard leaves, catches his train as usual and settles to work at his desk. There is some tentative knocking.

Triard. Come in Brian, I'm not going to eat you.

Brian. Good morning sir. I heard about the taxi. Nice repartee, sir. I can never think of the right thing to say until later.

Triard. Yes. It might be nice in general to think a bit before refraining from saying it. Now, in the

	absence of George Plate there are one or two things to sort out, but first - no more absenteeism.
Brian.	No, sir.
Triard.	But I have thought about what you said and agree that there may be something to be said for the occasional informal get together. I'll discuss it with the other partners. Now to matters of work. While George is in Scotland, he should go to Achnapond, so please get a message to him about it. Apparently they want a dolphin pile for their roll-on roll-off facility to turn on. Contact the harbourmaster for further information.
Brian.	Right. I think George is due at our Scottish office today. I'll get a message through to him there by phone or telex. One of these days we'll be able to carry personal phones with us.
Triard.	Doubtless. More overheads I suppose. Now - two: you're on the Westshire RDC work now, aren't you? Taken over from Vernon. He's built good relations there, so don't spoil them.
Brian.	Yes, sir. I was planning to go to their New Works Committee meeting on Wednesday. It looks like there's more work in the offing.
Triard.	Good, but there won't be unless you solve the business of the Monk Street smell. A small thing like that can permanently end a good relationship. What's the position with it?

Brian. Well, I discussed this with George last week, and we have a double banked solution. I have already arranged for a vent column and a sealed cover to the offending manhole which would have been connected by now, but George thinks the problem may be due to an air valve at the top of the rising main from Little Shortham where it discharges into the down hill drain. I got the RE to close it on Saturday and we shall just have to see. If the problem is not solved, I don't know what we can do short of a giant Airwick.

Triard. My God. I hope it doesn't come to that. Three: you may have heard that we have a new job in a more or less deserted island in the Mediterranean. It's to provide a sewage disposal facility for a projected resort development. I would have liked George Plate to deal with it, but

Brian. He's got a lot on his plate already.

Triard. I detect a certain amount of levity in your make-up, Brian, it needs controlling.

Brian. Yes, sir, sorry sir.

Triard. In that case, I think you should take it on. It will need a survey. According to the Client, there's an old 200 ft. shaft near the rock face which goes right down to below sea level. The Client is anxious that the discharge does not discolour the clear blue sea. Trouble is even clean freshwater shows up. It needs some thought, but in principle being wholly domestic sewage I think the best solution is a septic tank and clinker filter with intermittent syphonic discharge. It would not need much maintenance, a visit every two or three months from HQ on the main-land should be enough. You could set someone onto the design of the tank now - here's the designed population and water consumption data. Assume top water level is a foot or two above ground level. Further details, especially for the filter will have to wait on the survey. When do you think you could fit that in? I rather think they want the work finished next summer so that they can prepare for the next holiday season.

Brian. Would a few days after Christmas be too far away?

Triard. No, I don't think so as long as it's immediately after. Good. I'll let the Client know, so that he can make preliminary arrangements for accommodation, transport and general help - chainman and the like. Well, that's all I think, unless you have anything else.

Brian. Only one thing, sir. The draw-off tunnel using second hand cast-iron segments is in position at the reservoir site. Would you like to make a visit? It's at an interesting stage ready for the embankment fill and the puddle clay core.

Triard. Hm. Good idea. Thursday morning would be very convenient, especially because I'm giving evidence that afternoon at an arbitration on a tube failure. Yes, I could make something out of it. Sort it out for me please.

Brian. Very good, sir. Pick up from the office about 9.30?

Triard. Yes, fine. Give me time to check on the post. Now off you go.

* * * * *

Back at the borrow pit there is a large flooded area with a boat on it with two men in it. Two cars are parked in the background. Doreen, Jewel and Kelvin are on the bank.

Doreen. Well, John, here we are for our depth survey. Have you used a plane table before? - *John nods* - You'll see we've got ranging rods all round. Kelvin and chippy have set them up on a sort of regular grid. Kelvin, are you listening?

Kelvin. Yeah.

Doreen. I want you and Chippy to get the boat to the intersection of each grid and put the extended staff on the bottom. When you are ready, raise your arm each time and try to keep the staff upright. John, I suggest you set your table over there by my car, and I'll set mine up here so that we get a reasonable angle on each point.

John. OK. Seems alright. When I've got the direction plotted and have read the level, I'll raise my right arm. If there's a problem I'll raise my left.

Doreen. Right. No, left. When I've finished, I'll wave my right arm and, Kelvin, when you see that move to the next intersection on the same grid line.

Kelvin. Got it.

Doreen. Finish all the points on one grid line before moving to the next.

John. And Kelvin, I've no objection if you rest the staff on your foot.

Kelvin. Very funny. - *John sets up his table and moves over to help Doreen -*

John. Need a hand. I must say you look particularly attractive today.

Doreen. Now keep your mind on the job. - *she turns, trips over the instrument case. John catches her and holds a little longer than necessary - without too much resistance -*

While the survey continues, Brian Sheet arrives at the reservoir and starts to get off his gear. Noble meets him at the door of his office.

Noble. Morning Brian. How goes the battle?

Brian. To the strong, but what about you - and is young John OK?

Noble.	Yes. Hang on while I get some tea.

He goes into the hut and comes out with two mugs while Brian looks out over the site. There is a large area with all topsoil removed, a trench along the centre-line of the dam and a large tunnel, exposed, about 15 ft diameter, some two-thirds of it above present ground level.

Brian.	Thanks. Things are moving on aren't they?

Noble.	Yes. The good weather has been a great help. We shall be starting on the puddle clay core soon. Yes, John seems to have settled down well. The Contractor's site engineer, Doreen, has impressed him, possibly frightened him a little. We don't want propinquity to propink too much.

Brian.	Good, better keep an eye on it. These things can develop very suddenly. Anyhow, I came to have a general look-see and to discuss a visit proposed by Sir Triard. Would Thursday morning be OK? I know he wants to look at the tunnel in particular, but has to be away by lunch time latest.

Noble.	Yes, I'm sure that's OK. The clay pug mill will be working by then and it would save time to get his opinion, as 'The Engineer'. Let me show you round.

They put their mugs down inside the door, Brian puts on his knee boots, and they wander off towards the tunnel.

* * * * *

Brian Sheet's house is not on main drainage so he has to order partial emptying of the septic tank every now and then. Today, a sludge gulper, half hidden by flies, is on the drive, and the operator finishes stowing the hose. Frances Sheet looks frustrated at her apple press and goes up to the operator.

Frances.   Sorry to bother you. Gods, what a smell!

Operator.   Sorry about that. Won't hang around for long. What can I do for you?

Frances.   Well it's this damned apple press. I can't seem to release the jack.

The operator goes and looks at it and, with his heavy duty gloves on, releases the pressure.

Operator.   No problem, nice jack but a bit over the top for this press.

Frances.   Thanks so much. I don't know what the smell will do to the juice. We're going to ferment it for apple wine.

Operator.   Good idea. Lasts better than Apple Jack. I shouldn't worry about the smell. Might give it a little body so to speak! Well, I must be off.

He goes to the gulper, gets in and backs it out of the drive, Frances waving.

* * * * *

The Westshire RDC New Works Committee is in session.

Chairman. Shall we call in Mr Sheet? Estelle?

Estelle. By all means.

Chairman. Mr Clerk, can you get him in, please. – *the Clerk opens the door and beckons* – Welcome Mr Sheet, how do you do?

Brian. Fine thanks Mr Chairman, but a bit fearful.

Chairman. Why is that?

Brian. The Monk Street smell, sir; have you anything to report?

Chairman. Monk Street smell, eh.. Mrs Humphrey-Jones have you anything to report to the committee?

Estelle. Yes, Chairman. I have myself visited the site early on several mornings and have consulted residents and shop-keepers in that area. The summary of my findings has been put in writing to the Council's Clerk – *who nods* –

Chairman. Yes of course, but can you summarise it for us now and for information of Mr Sheet?

Estelle. Chairman, well as I was saying I have personally investigated the site of the smell and have spoken to our Surveyor..

Chairman. Yes, yes, but no need to spin it out now. Mr Sheet is growing more nervous by the minute.

Estelle. Sorry, Chairman, no-one has detected any sewage smell in the last month.

Chairman. Well, Mr Sheet, what have you to say and what would you have done had it been otherwise?

Brian. Thank you very much, sir; that's a great relief, and if it's not out of order I would like to stand Mrs Humphrey-Jones a drink at the Bull this evening.

Chairman. I'll leave that to Mrs Humphrey-Jones, but it is rather out of order at this meeting. But for interest's sake and possible future use, what would you have done?

Brian. I discussed this briefly with Sir Triard and apart from completely re-routing the sewer etc the only thing we could think of was a giant Airwick.

Chairman. Ye Gods.

Brian. Yes, that's what Sir Triard said, but it has been used, I think, on the leeward side of a sewage works - Bletchley, I think.

Chairman. Enough of this. According to my notes, there are two other matters, the Square Grove Sewage Works and the house connections where survey is complete. Oh. Yes, and thirdly, we are getting a number of claims for damages where sewers and pumping mains have gone through private property.

Clerk. There seems to have been some sort of collusion, possibly using the same solicitor, but they all come under the heading 'injurious affection'.

Chairman. We've done all we are supposed to have done, I hope, notices in due time and form, photographs before and after etc.?

Clerk. Yes, sir; all were served notices under the relevant Section of the 1936 Public Health Act, but there is the question whether we should counterclaim for betterment.

Chairman. That's an idea. Can't we claim betterment everywhere? After all, they now have water and drainage services which they didn't have before.

Clerk. Not really, sir. As I read the Act, you can't claim betterment unless it's a counterclaim for damages, but I suppose we could hold that in the background if it comes to the crunch with claimants.

Chairman. Just as well. It wouldn't have gone down too well with the voters. Yes, Mr Sheet?

Brian. Your RE, Mr Blander, has been kept informed by the Council's Clerk and has kept a note of the after effects. There are one or two justifiable claims for physical damage to walls and the odd fruit

	tree, but generally speaking where trenches have been dug across cultivated land their location can be seen by a line of better crops, or lusher grass.
Chairman.	Well Mr Clerk, make sure that this is all recorded so that it can be evidenced in court if it comes to that, but I'm sure that with your tact and Mr Sheet's sense of humour you should be able to avoid that. Within the limit of our budget for petty cash you may find some assistance at the Bull. Worth a little expense to keep the troops happy, I mean the voters not the Consulting Engineer. Now, Mr Sheet, what about the other matters?
Brian.	As to house connections, sir, the main problem is surface water run-off from rear of properties – roofs and drives – which has been connected to foul sewers, illegally, I may say. The problem won't arise from the new schemes if publicity and a good watch is given for DIY enthusiasts. We have more or less completed a survey of Greenway and have found a large proportion of properties illegally connected, including, I may say that of the Public Health Inspector - *chuckles all round* - probably done before he bought the house.
Chairman.	Quite so.
Brian.	Finally, as to the Square Grove Sewage Works, we have completed the outline design and form for submission to the Ministry. I've got it with me and will give it to your Clerk after this. When you

have submitted it, I think you can expect a notice for a local inquiry - unless of course you get a lot of objections when the Minister may decide on a public inquiry.

Chairman. Good, and thank you, but we are familiar with Ministry procedures. We'll let you know what's decided upon in due course. Now, Mr Sheet, we have appreciated your attendance at our meetings. It has been most helpful, but unless anything crops up I don't think you need to plan to attend any more for the time being.

Brian. Thank you very much, sir. Given reasonable notice, I can make sure I or a colleague will be able to attend when required. And thank you, sir, and your committee for your attention.

He bows out

* * * * *

Outside RE's office at the reservoir site, Noble, Sir Triard, Jewel and Brian stand in a group.

Noble. Well, Sir Triard, I think the climb might have tired you a little. Anyhow tea is on the way.

Triard. Not at all, but site tea will be welcome - in a decent sized mug, not those damned little things my wife uses. Anyhow, I would like to see a sample of the clay, and can we have the Agent or

	his site engineer here at the time?
Noble.	Jewel, can you pop over and get Mr Isles to come; I know he is standing by. - *Jewel leaves at the double and Kelvin enters -*
Kelvin.	Here's the bucket of clay you wanted.
Noble.	Thanks very much. - *Kelvin leaves and a site inspector enters with mugs of tea, bowl of sugar, spoon and biscuits -* Thanks Eric. - *Jewel arrives with the site Agent, Mr Isles. Eric hands out the tea and disappears -*
Triard.	Hello, Isles, glad to see you again. Can't remember where it was. East London sewage works, I think. How are you keeping?
Isles.	Quite right, sir. I'm fine and enjoying this contract - not quite so demanding as that rather large sewage works, but technically more interesting for me, and how about you?
Triard.	Much the same, I suppose, and all the better for being on site. Now, let's have a look at this clay. There are some fairly sophisticated tests for it depending on what Standard Specification is used, generally BS or ASSHO. - Noble, you had better get some sent to the Building Research Station and say we are using the BS tests - but on the practical side there's no better test than to roll it between your hands to produce a half inch diameter roll and throw it at a wall. If it sticks, it's

OK - like this. - *Triard, Isles and Noble do this for a little to the amazement of Jewel who laughs -*

Triard. Well that looks OK; we need not hold the work up until we get the test results. What are you laughing at, young man?

Jewel. Sorry, sir, I came on site for practical experience. I seem to be getting it.

Triard. Hm! Good. Now, Noble, and Isles for that matter, I walked through the tunnel, which seems generally satisfactory considering that the segments are second hand, but we don't want the tunnel to leak more than cannot be helped. The bolt grommets look a bit hit and miss and need attention. But I am more concerned about possible seepage along the outside skin, and the water stop flange you've put in looks very floppy and fragile, likely to tear easily. You'll have to stop it splitting when the clay is puddled round it.

Isles. Yes, Sir Triard, I'll get some sort of timber framework to hold it in place.

Triard. Good. Noble, you'll watch it of course because it's very difficult to control piping after completion. Thank you for the tea. Now, Brian, let's get away. I've got to be at an arbitration hearing this afternoon.

Triard and Brian go, leaving Isles, Noble and Jewel rolling and throwing clay sausages with abandon.

* * * * *

After a quick lunch at St Stephen's Club, Sir Triard goes to the arbitration room. The arbitrator is at a table with piles of bundles of documents and books at a side table. Counsel and solicitor for the defence are at a table to his left with those for the plaintiff on his right. Beyond counsel is a desk with Sir Triard sitting behind it, in the box as it is called. Counsel for the plaintiff rises to question him and Sir Triard stands.

Counsel. Sir Triard, we are looking forward to hearing your evidence, which, as you know, is to help this court not to further your client's case.

Triard. I understand, but I hope you are not suggesting that I withhold my opinions in favour of my client.

Counsel. Of course not, as long as you don't withhold opinions which may not help your client. Good. Now your proof of evidence, see page 203 in the bundle in front of you, stipulates the various tunnel projects with which you have been concerned, but the last one was some years ago, and, if I may say so, aren't you a bit old for this sort of work and wouldn't you prefer to sit down? I'm sure the court would be understanding. So it may be supposed that you are not currently involved with up-to-date experience in the arduous work of investigating segmental tunnel work.

Triard. No, you may not say so, no I can stand perfectly well and no it is not so.

Counsel. But your proof does not refer to any recent work; so how can you say 'No'?

Triard. The proof was completed some months ago, and as is the nature of arbitrations conducted through lawyers, work continues during periods of delay.

Arbitrator. Sir Triard, I am not sure that your last observation answered the question and might be supposed to be a criticism of this court.

Triard. Oh, sir, I had no intention to criticise your conduct of the arbitration and apologise profoundly. I know myself how difficult it is to get the parties, especially if represented by lawyers, to keep to a tolerable programme, which I am sure you will have set at the beginning. We older ones do it better.

Arbitrator. Well, that's as may be, but please answer the question.

Triard. Thank you, sir, but it so happens that I was inspecting just such a tunnel only this morning.

Counsel. Please describe it.

Triard. It is a 15 foot diameter second hand cast iron segmental tunnel, just such as the tunnel subject of this claim.

Counsel. So, perhaps, you can describe the sort of defects which you saw or which might be expected in others.

Triard. I hope that you are not asking me to describe defects in the tunnel I inspected this morning.

Counsel. No, I'm sorry, I will rephrase the question. What sort of defects would you expect to see in a tunnel the nature of which is such as the subject of this arbitration?

Triard. Ah. That's better. - *the arbitrator wags his finger at Sir Triard* - Probably the most important thing to look for is distortion and cracking associated with reassembly. Other matters which one looks for include...- *the hearing continues* -

* * * * *

Back in Scotland on the West coast, on one of the quays of Achnapond harbour George Plate stands with Simon Callow of Scottish Ferries, John Donovan the harbour master and Jack Lemon the Customs and Excise officer.

Donovan. Mr Plate, can I call you George? - *George nods* - I'll leave it to Mr Callow to explain what we want.

George. Thanks Mr Donovan; can I call you Donnie? - after all we've been meeting for several years and everyone else calls you that.

Donovan. Of course; Jack Lemon is here just to satisfy himself that whatever is decided upon doesn't make his job more difficult.

George. Right, Mr Callow; haven't we met somewhere before? Ah. Yes; Kithwheel High Rise buildings wasn't it?

Callow. Quite right. Civil engineering is really quite a small world isn't it?

George. Yes. I understand that if you sit in Jeddah airport every day for a week you'll see all the engineers who work overseas. No matter; I understand from Mr Donovan's letter to head office that to make use of the roll-on roll-off ferry ramp you need a dolphin to help your new ferries berth stern to.

Callow. Yes. That's right. What we want is a turning dolphin at the quay approach about 20 yards off the end.

George. I don't see any difficulty in principle, but what sort do you have in mind?

Callow. Well, what we want is something which won't damage our ferries.

Donovan. And what we want is one which won't be damaged by your ferries, unless you indemnify us against such damage.

Callow. OK. But don't let's get carried away into insurances just yet; let's see what your consultant comes up with.

George. There are two major aspects, as I see it. The

	dolphin must be strong enough to withstand your ferry's approach, and we need to know its tonnage and maximum approach velocity. Secondly we will need to provide suitable protection.
Callow.	The ferry we shall be using is 900 tonnes displacement, and I think the approach velocity is unlikely to exceed five knots.
Donovan.	Five knots you say! For goodness sake are your skippers ex destroyer captains? The maximum cross tide here is no more than one knot.
George.	I think that the protection should be such as to inspire caution in your skippers; perhaps some rather visible iron bolt heads between vertical lengths of greenheart timbering?
Callow.	Perhaps we can limit approach velocity to two knots, but I really don't like the idea of these bolts.
Donovan.	I would like to see a fairly flexible construction and as many bolts as possible to deter the fishing boats from using it, otherwise it won't last any time. At the same time we don't want to involve the Harbour Board in more expense than necessary.
George.	Suppose we design the dolphin as a timber lattice construction, open to wave action to minimize design strength against wave action, and with iron bolts protruding on three sides and heavy duty, possibly revolving, neoprene fendering on the fourth side. Is that sort of approach agreeable?

Donovan. In principle I would agree, but Id like to see the outline design before going ahead in detail. I certainly like the idea of timber construction rather than the usual steel, so that damaged timber, presumably greenheart, can be replaced using port facilities.

Callow. Again, in principle, I also agree, and could Mr Plate send me a copy of what he sends you, Mr Donovan - *Donovan nods* -

George. OK. I'll get the design criteria stipulated in writing together with an outline of the design itself. Basically, it's 900 tonnes and, to give a little margin of safety, at no more than two and a half knots, direct or glancing.

Callow. Agreed. Now I must buzz off. Good to meet you again Mr Plate and I look forward, Mr Donovan, to early implementation. We want to get the new ferry into operation as soon as possible.

Donovan. Good. We'll do the best we can. - *Callow leaves* - Now, George, any more ideas?

George. No, I don't think so, except perhaps that you put in some fairly forbidding warning signs at appropriate locations, but your Board must realize that a really robust dolphin would be very expensive and the proposed flexible one may raise your insurer's eyebrows.

Donovan. Yes I'll get them to take that on board, but we'll try to get a suitable indemnity from Scottish Ferries, and we'll give some preliminary notice of intention to the Admiralty and Trinity House. Now, Lemon old chap, I believe you've got something to show George.

Lemon. Yes, come over here a bit. - *they all move to the back of the quay* - I have saved some scampi from the Russian trawler's visit yesterday. Would you like some? - *he picks one out of an ice kettle* -

George. Gods! It's gigantic, more like a young lobster. I'd love to take two or three home, if that's OK.

Lemon. No, you don't see them like this in UK. All the best ones go abroad, mostly to Spain, but no problem. I'll get them packed in ice and sent directly to your home by courier.

George Well, thanks very much indeed. That will be best as I've got to spend a few more days up here before going home. I'll warn my wife they are coming and to stick them in the coldest part of the fridge.

Lemon. That's right but no deep freeze, you know.

George. Thanks, you two. I'll get someone onto the estimate early next week, Donnie, and look forward to seeing you both soon. Can't offer you lunch today; I have to be at the Firth Council offices this afternoon. - *hand shakes all round and George goes off to his car* -

Later at the Firth District Council office. Sitting and chatting round a table are Euan Fairway, Janet Dropshot, (Flash) Harry Smart, Mr Plank his QS and the Chief Engineer Mr Ian Astair.

Flash.   Now, look here, this is ridiculous and I'm not standing for it. We do a good job and you throw the book at us over a small extra.

Astair.   Mr Smart, please calm down; it's not a small extra, but let's wait for - ah. Here he is.

George.   *enters.* Hello all. I'm sorry I'm late and do apologise. I was at Achnapond this morning for an unplanned visit and miscalculated the speed I would maintain over the narrow roads. Enough to send one round the bend.

Fairway.   It llllooks as if the afternoon wwwill keep you round the bbbend.

George.   Now, Euan, let's wait on the event.

Janet.   Tomorrow and tomorrow and tomorrow creeps on this petty pace.

George.   Oh, Janet, I'm too tired for that, and, anyhow, what are you doing here?

Astair.   Flash, Mr Smart, asked me to have her here if possible as she was in at the time of the tender/contract stage. I'm not quite sure why, because it's all a matter of words in writing.

Janet. In the beginning was the ..

George. Quiet, Janet. Mr Astair, could we start with you?

Janet. Sorry, I am mute and will not speak a word.

George. Good. To continue, it might help if you set the scene as-it-were and then we can ask Mr Smart to make his case.

Astair. Well, it's all really simple. The contractor was asked to tender for your pre-designed crossing of the canal during its decennial closure using sheet steel piling to the design approved by the Regional Engineer, but given the option to do the work in tunnel if he wished, but at the tendered price for the canal closure work. His tender was qualified because it asked for an extra if the cost of steel piling went up if he had to buy abroad because British Steel couldn't supply in time. We admit that supply from British Steel was uncertain. Janet, here, in discussion with me drafted a condition for inclusion in the letter of acceptance which limited the extra cost. Janet, can you read the actual words.

Janet. Yes, it goes 'Your tender is accepted subject to an increase of not exceeding £10 per square yard for sheet piling in the event that it could not be bought in time from British Steel Corporation'.

Astair. We sent this to MacAllwork for their approval. They agreed, subject to deletion of 'not exceeding'.

After some inquiry of British Steel and the Belgian market, I agreed to the change and the letter of acceptance went out accordingly. The Contractor got on with the work, but chose to do the crossing in tunnel. He is claiming the £10 extra rate even though he didn't use steel piling. We see no reason why he should succeed. I may say we have had some stormy correspondence before setting up this meeting, and I hope you can resolve it; by the way this is to be an Engineer's decision.

George. Thank you, Mr Astair, for your clear presentation. My impression is that your intention at the time was that if the Contractor chose not to use steel piling then the tendered rates would apply.

Astair. Yes, that's just it.

George. Now Mr Smart, it's your turn.

Flash. I'm sorry, Mr Plate, I'm not really composed enough to argue lucidly, and, if you permit, I will ask Plank to continue. I believe you know him

George. No problem. Mr Plank, please go ahead.

Plank. Well, Mr Plate, it seems to me pretty simple. We had the option to use a tunnel. In deciding this option we had to balance its cost against the cost of trenching, which would have included the extra cost of the steel piling. I think the Council agree that this would have been incurred. *George looks at Astair.*

Astair. Yes. There certainly would have been an extra, but we are not sure that it would have been as much as £10. But that's not the point. The Contractor did not use steel piling and on the strict wording of his tender qualification 'that if he had to get piles other than from BSC the item for sheet piling should be increased by £10 per square yard' he shouldn't receive it.

Plank. But Mr Plate, sorry, this was prior to contract. The actual contract makes no such condition; it just provides for an extra price if piles could not be got from BSC in time. It is agreed that that is the case.

George. Mr Astair, it does seem as though the Contractor has a case. To my mind the only area of doubt is whether the tender qualification is admissible for interpreting the contract.

Astair. I'm bound to say I'm disappointed at what you are saying, but where do we go from here?

George. I can't give, or rather ask Sir Triard, to give an Engineer's decision until I'm sure on the question of admissibility of the tender qualification, so if you and Mr Smart can't agree on it, I suggest that we put the matter to a Writer to the Signet rather than going straight away to the expense of arbitration on the Engineer's decision and that we abide by what he says. Do you both agree?

Flash. Yes, it does seem to boil down to what you say, so that with some confidence I agree. What do you say, Mr Astair?

Astair. It does look as though it's a sensible option, but I don't know how the Council will take it.

George. I don't think they should worry at this stage, because it is agreed that whatever the Writer says will be the basis of the Engineer's decision under Clause 66, so that at that stage if either party is aggrieved they can always go to arbitration.

Astair. Yes, of, course, I had forgotten about that. OK go ahead.

George. In that case it would be as well if the minutes of this meeting were signed by both parties as agreed. While we adjourn for polite conversation - and perhaps some tea, Mr Astair - Janet can tidy up her notes into a presentable form for signature. - Can't you Janet?

Janet. Yes, George, it shouldn't take too long - so hallowed and gracious is the time, then weary with toil I'll haste me to my bed.

George. Thanks, now …

The tea comes in, a cup is put before Janet, and the rest move away talking.

Next morning in a very modern and well furnished room in

Firth Regional Council's new office block, George Plate and Milroy, an accountant, sit in chairs before a desk at which the Chief Engineer, Iain Astare, is sitting.

George. Good to see you, Mr Astare, thanks for finding the time. How are you keeping?

Astare. Well, thank you, as I hope it finds you.

George. I find it very confusing that your name is much the same as that of the Chief Engineer of Firth District Council.

Astare. That's as may be but we Scots find no difficulty in distinguishing us. It's all in the pronunciation, you see.

George. You must teach me some day, but

Astare. I'm sorry to rush you, Mr Plate, but I've got another meeting to prepare for. What do you want this time?

George. To come to the point, then, why are you not paying our last bill?

Astare. I thought that would be it. Milroy here can explain.

Milroy. The fact is, the Chief Finance Officer was asked by the Chairman of Council to examine the fees and expenses we have been paying you, and he asked me to look at them.

George. So?

Milroy. So, they are far in excess of the budget for them, and that's what he reported to Council.

Astare. And as I have to certify payment, I was instructed not to certify any more.

George. But I cannot be responsible for your budgeting. We've done the work and billed in accordance with the agreement.

Astare. Yes, I know, but the agreement was based on your report and the estimates as agreed by Council.

George. Really, this is not tolerable. You're worse than the Roads and Bridges Corporation of I'd better not say where.

Astare. Mr Plate, we have had a lot of trouble with other Consultants over-charging.

George. But we are not other Consultants. What is obviously wrong is that your budget was fixed in stone as soon as we got the job and has not been adjusted to take account of inflation, much of it as a result of delay in letting the construction contracts.

Astare. Milroy, what do you say to that?

Milroy. I don't know. All I was asked to do was to check against the budget, and just as well because it

	should have been checked before. Expenditure is way over the top.
Astare.	Look, Mr Plate, why don't you come to the next Council meeting and make an explanation?
George.	Certainly, that's a good idea, and thanks for the opportunity. I am confident that both the cost of the works, on which our fee is based, and the salary cost of supervising staff have not exceeded over-all estimates adjusted for inflation. I will prepare an analysis for projection in your splendid new Council chamber.
Astare.	Good, I am sorry that this problem has arisen and hope you can convince Council. There have been critical articles in the press which they had to take note of.
George.	It looks as though there's a snake in the grass with an axe to grind to coin a phrase.
Astare.	You may be right at that. But enough of this. What do you think of our new building?
George.	From what I've seen it seems very good and planned with future expansion in mind?
Astare.	Yes. We have had to consider and provide for an emergency control centre, but it's all complete now, except for the logo to go above the entrance door. Members of Council cannot agree on it.

George.   Have you thought of a sixpence?

Astare.   Now, now Mr Plate, but I must go now. Let's have a dram this evening?

CHAPTER 6

TALKING TURKEY

It is again a Monday morning in Lady Sylvia's kitchen.

Triard. Well, dear, I suppose I had better get going.

Sylvia. You don't really want to go, do you?

Triard. You're probably right, but I've got a lot on.

Sylvia. What you need is more help at a senior level. Have you thought any more about it?

Triard. Of course I have. It's one of my bigger worries - to get the succession settled so that financial considerations can be given time for a smooth handover.

Sylvia. Well, what about George Plate? You seem to think highly of him.

Triard. Yes. He's certainly partner material, but the other partners are reluctant to rock the boat.

Sylvia. Well isn't there some way of getting them used to him and getting confidence in him?

Triard. I think so as you suggest, but slowly, slowly, and it's no use him continuing to work for me on my projects for my clients. I rely on him heavily as it is. The other partners won't get to know him that way.

Sylvia.   If only you could make your mind up, you'd feel better immediately. Forget about your projects; cometh the hour cometh the man.

Triard.   You are probably right, as usual. I shall have to let him go to another partner, I suppose, but only when he's finished one or two outstanding jobs.

Sylvia.   Good, stick to that - you'll feel better at once. Who could replace him?

Triard.   There are one or two competent in the offing, but rather immature at present.

Sylvia.   If you give them more responsibility, they'll mature quickly enough.

Triard.   Perfectly right again, my dear; you're a great help. I'll start the ball rolling with the other partners and give them time to get used to the idea of change. The trouble is they are a good bit younger than I am. Anyhow, I think I'll treat myself to a good lunch at St Stephen's club and let George sort out any emergencies; although when he's around there don't seem to be many. Good chap. We must have him and his wife round for a meal one day.

Sylvia.   If you say so, dear, but don't get ahead of yourself.

Triard.   This is getting boring, but right again, I'm bound to say. I must be off now; I've already missed the 8.15, but in a good cause. Back as usual.

Sylvia.   Good bye, love. - *kisses him as he leaves* -

He goes straight to his office, looks through some post and sends for George, who arrives promptly.

George.   You're looking pleased for a Monday morning, if I may say so.

Triard.   Good heavens. Is it so obvious? Well, I've made a decision I've put off for some time.

George.   It does help, doesn't it. I've got a decision to make, too.

Triard.   Don't say you are thinking of leaving us.

George.   What? No, of course not, but these contracts in the south-west are growing, with two potentially difficult contractors. As you know, John Jewel has moved from the reservoir job where he was assistant to the RE for about a year. He's now RE on the Pump Station job and the tunnel sewer job, which has just started. You remember approving the move? - *Sir Triard nods* - He's only had a year's experience on site and is not really ready for the full responsibilities of an Engineer's Representative, even if we gave him limited powers. And if we did, he could be unduly open to pressure from the contractors. I think I'll have to spend a good bit of detailed time on them, if you agree, with plenty of visits. There might be a time when a visit from you would be helpful. A little heavyweight can do a lot of good by being there.

Triard. I agree, They are both important jobs, and big ones at that, but I hope you're not going to ask me to visit as a sort of bystander in a top hat. It must be so that I can contribute something. Time is short enough as it is.

George. Of course, but it does mean that more will be pushed onto Brian Sheet. Might cure his levity a bit at that.

Triard. Good thinking. Yes. That might be a good idea for the long term. Well, let me know how you get on. Off you go now.

* * * * *

Brian decides that he needs to make a positive effort to keep fit. He goes jogging before breakfast on a footpath. Where it joins a road at a bus shelter, one day, he comes across a small boy smoking. Brian Sheet jogs up and stops.

Brian. You'll never run a four minute mile if you go on smoking.

Boy. I know, but the girls expect you to smoke.

Brian. What about the girls who don't smoke?

Boy. I don't know none like that.

Brian. Well, it's up to you, but why not look for one who doesn't smoke. Tastes nicer when snogging..

Brian finishes his jog, has a shower, a quick breakfast and roars off to the station on his motor bike, ending up in his design office, which is full of workers working. George enters.

George. Morning all. Brian, a minute if you can spare it. – *they move to a corner desk and sit down* – You're looking disgustingly healthy.

Brian. Good. I've taken up jogging before breakfast. I seem to be able to last the day better.

George. Well, you may have to jog at lunch time, too, because we're making some changes.

Brian. Ring in the new, what?

George. Yes, a sort of musical chairs.

Brian. Very good. So what are they?

George. I'm going to have to spend much, if not all, of my time on the South West contracts with a bit of Scotland thrown in from time to time, which will leave a bit of a gap on other work, and that's where you come in.

Brian. Sounds interesting. What do you want me to do?

George. Well, Sir T thought it time for you to take on more responsibility. So you are to report directly to him on all work related to the Rural Water & Sewerage Act.

Brian.   That's good, but what about the reservoir?

George.   Oh. Yes - to include seeing to the winding up of that contract - final account and as-built drawings in cooperation with Bob Noble until he finds another job or is given one.

Brian.   OK. That should fill my time nicely.

George.   And by the way - Sir T thought the increased responsibility might help to curb untimely levity - muffling the bells as-it-were.

Brian.   Message understood, but between ourselves a bit of humour helps to get through the day.

George.   Of course. It's just a matter of discretion, not valour. We all have our way; for example, Janet quotes Shakespeare, more and more as the end of the week approaches. I once caught her late on a Friday at the copying machine saying aloud 'for God's sake let us sit upon the ground and tell sad stories of the death of kings' or some such. Anyhow, if anything seriously bothers you. You can always get hold of me. So, cheers, I'm off to bonnie Scotland now. Miss Firesmoke will usually know where I am.

George waves all round and leaves for his journey, and eventually arrives at Achnapond Harbour, where on the ferry quay he greets John Donovan harbourmaster, Jack Lemon Customs and Excise, and Simon Callow Scottish Ferries.

Callow.   There you are Mr Plate. A ruined dolphin first time used.

George.   It certainly looks a bit sick. Donny, can you tell me what happened?

Donavan.   Yes, I was watching to see how it went…

Lemon.   And I was watching - for contraband and any necessary precautions for the future.

George.   Good. I hope you've written down what you both saw - separately, I hope. Now tell me what happened.

Donovan.   Well, the ferry approached as expected, doing about 2 to 2½ knots.

Callow.   Yes, the skipper says he was doing a touch over 2 knots.

Donovan.   It came alongside the dolphin before turning on it, and the dolphin leant over quite a bit, but when the ferry stopped turning the dolphin did not recover. I went to look at it in my dory, afterwards, and two of the main timbers have cracked. It wouldn't be too much of a problem replacing them as the design allows, but I wouldn't want to do that if every time the ferry comes in the same thing happens. It looks as though the basic design is wrong, Mr Plate, and I and the Board would look to you to do a redesign and replacement at no cost to the Board as I am sure you will understand.

George.   I see, or I don't see. I'm sure the design met the specification - but was insurance in place?

Donovan.   No, I'm afraid not. The insurers wanted to see how it worked under normal conditions. Fortunately, they didn't see it happen, and I haven't informed them, waiting on the result of this meeting.

George.   Mr Callow, as I recall your requirements as agreed with Mr Donovan, they were that the dolphin should be fairly flexible and able to stand up to a 900 ton ferry approaching with 2 knots impact velocity. Agreed?

Callow.   Yes, that's right.

George.   What was the ferry's name?

Donovan.   Anois. I hadn't seen it before on this route, and noted the name particularly. I looked it up in Lloyds Register of shipping before agreeing to it on this route. It said 950 tons, and I didn't think that was outside normal factors of safety and said go ahead.

George.   Mr Callow, is that right? And where was it normally used?

Callow.   This was its maiden voyage. We needed to test demand for capacity.

George.   You mean it was bigger.

Callow. Yes a bit. I expected this sort of question and brought along the shipbuilder's summary. Have a look at it, with pleasure. - *he hands a folder to George, who takes it,, and reads for a bit -*

George. But it says here that it is 1450 tons. That's more than 50% bigger than the design specification. You can't possibly say that's within normal factors of safety.

Donovan. But Lloyds Register said 950 tons.

George. I'm very sorry to say, Donny, that you should have looked at the manufacturer's description. There's a very frightening case precedent which is directly applicable. You all should read it; it is Howard Marine and Ogden, Court of Appeal, year before last, I think. Anyhow, I think that you and the Board should discuss the matter with Scottish Ferries, ascertain what revision to the specification is necessary and instruct us what to do. At this stage I'm certainly not accepting any liability for the firm.

Donovan. Hm. That's plain enough. When we've agreed with Scottish Ferries what is needed, I'll let you know, but we may be able to improve the strength locally if necessary - after all the foundations appear undamaged. We must look to our purse ye ken.

George. Or that of Scottish Ferries. If you do decide to do it yourself, I'd be glad to check your proposals for a nominal fee.

Donovan. How much?

George. How about a dozen scampi; I'm sure Sir Triard would like one or two.

Donovan. Done -*they shake hands, then George shakes hands with the others and turns to his car* –

Callow. I'll get our MD to contact you, Mr Donovan, to fix a meeting. We don't want this facility to be out of action any longer than necessary.

Donovan. Right, Mr Callow, we'll be waiting.

* * * * *

In the South West, work has started at the site where the pump station is being built together with its outfall pipeline. John Jewel is the resident engineer (RE) and in his office he is at a drawing board with Jack Paul, one of the Contractor's engineers.

Paul. What I've come to talk about is the design of the temporary works for the tidal outfall, and this is our design. - *Jewel studies it* –

Jewel. So, basically, you're adapting the provision of the permanent sheet piling but extending it upward, presumably to cut it off when complete.

Paul. Got it in one, although I believe from the Bill of Quantities that that was anticipated, but what I've come about is the provision against collapse at high tides.

	e. What flood level are you considering?
	Six inches above highest spring tide from the almanac.
Jewel.	Sounds alright, though I'm no expert on tides.
Paul.	Understood, but that's not the point; it has been set by the contracts manager. It's the method of strutting I want to discuss.
Jewel.	I'm not sure that's my interest as long as it doesn't affect our ability to inspect falsework and reinforcement during construction of the permanent work. - *he looks more closely* - No, that seems OK, although Alec may have to slim a bit. How are you getting on since changing sides?
Paul.	Well, I left Noplay & Partners after two and a bit years including one on site at the reservoir, you know.
Jewel.	Yes, interesting, but why?
Paul.	The construction was a bit limited, you know, mostly earthmoving and I wanted hands-on in a wider context, which I seem to be getting alright.
Jewel.	Good, but I'm not sure I would have done it that way; still all sorts. When's the pile driver getting here?
Paul.	Next Monday. He's said to be one of the old

school – worked most of his life on flood defences. Brings his own boiler and bits and pieces and puts it all together himself – won't let anyone else touch it. Should be worth watching. Apparently he drinks heavily every day after work and turns up promptly the next morning fresh as a rather wrinkled daisy.

Jewel. I'll look forward to seeing him. What's he called?

Paul. I don't know his real name. You'll be able to get it from the pay sheets, but he is usually referred to as Steam Hammer Bill, but sometimes as Cirrhosis of the River.

Jewel. I think I'd better call him Bill. OK, be seeing you.

Some days later, Jewel visits the Outfall site. Bill is having a cuppa. He's a bit on the deaf side. It looks like a junk yard. A rather old crane has a steel pile hooked on and partly raised. Some timber framing is erected each side of the outfall beyond four piles which have already been driven. The boiler is steaming and hissing.

Jewel. *loudly* Morning Bill, how's it going?

Bill. Orlright, thanks, Engineer.

Jewel. So what's happening? Come on, I want to learn, not to criticise.

Bill. Well, I got the end four piles stitched an' driven each side as you can see. 'Ad a bit of bother this

	side – there's some sort of thin rock or slate on a slope and the toes kept slipping.
Jewel.	So what did you do? I see the frame sets the piles about half way up.
Bill.	Yeah, no problem. I bounced the piles until they penetrated – upright as you see. I'll say this tide is a big one, more than I'm used to, must be 15 ft or so. It'll help setting the piles at low tide but could be a nuisance keeping the frame in place at high tide.
Jewel.	Why not attach the landward end to the last pile driven?
Bill.	Yeah. I'll have a word with a chippy about that – but the tide won't put any stress on the piles until I close off the end. Before then, they'll have to be strutted.
Jewel.	What's that in the water?
Bill.	Only a dead sheep. Passes the site four times a day.
Jewel.	Can't be much fresh in the river. Have you seen the bore?
Bill.	Nah. It's neaps at the moment an' won't be springs for a for'night. I'll have closed the coffer by then. OK now? I'll start stitching the next four.
Jewel.	Good. Can I take a message back for you? You

could do with a phone line down here.

Bill. Nah. Don't want no phone. Couldn't hear it anyroad - but yes, ask the agent to send down a chippy and some gas cutting gear.

Jewel. OK. Be seeing you.

Jewel stays a few minutes to watch the stitching in progress, then waves at Bill and returns to the main site.

* * * * *

On his way to the pump station site, George stops to visit a small job at Force & Co.s brewery on the way. He is directed upstairs to the RE's office. It is a very nice room with oak panelling, good furniture, and a beer pump in one corner. One leaded window looks out over a stone lined channel, full of trout, at the edge of the street. The opposite window looks out over the cask yard and doors to the cooperage. Janet is standing, and George looks round admiringly.

George. I was told you were down here? And you seem to have got yourself well set up. Very good to see you again, but I thought you were settled at the Hydro Scheme.

Janet. A woman in her time plays many parts, you know. It's a longish story, but seeking the bubble reputation you might say.

George. Gods, you're still not at it are you?

Janet. And why not? Anyhow, as I was saying, I applied for a job advertised round the firm for an RE in East Africa, and Sir Triard arranged a replacement. This is a short job to fill in time until I set off. I'm not sure Mr Bridgeman was too happy about it, but Vernon was getting very useful.

George. Good, glad to hear it; I must make a visit soon. So which partner will you be working for?

Janet. Andrew Ingleton. Seems alright. He said I might have some bother with the locals to start with and to make sure I looked as unattractive as possible and well covered.

George. I don't like the sound of that or the sight, for that matter. Still, this is an informal visit, suggested by Sir Triard, to see if you have any problems.

Janet. No. It's all fairly straight forward. We're putting in a settling tank over there. It's much smaller than I'm used to, but Sir T said the spent hops drop out very quickly. Talking of hops, have a beer?

George. Good heavens, does that work? They ARE looking after you.

Janet. We'll teach you to drink deep ere you depart. Yes, the chief brewer thought I ought to have it. Shouldn't be much difficulty in arranging site meetings.

George. I'm not sure Sir Triard would approve, and I would be inclined to keep quiet about it; although he does seem to have a lighter mood these days.

Janet. Perhaps in these cups I shall be freshly remembered, anyhow.

George. At least you seem to have plenty of time to "brush up your Shakespeare" - have you seen 'Kiss me Kate'? No matter.

Janet. While you are here, perhaps you could have a look at my proposed route for the rising main to the tank. Part of it goes through a culvert under the brewery - full of trout which must not be frightened under pain of removing my beer pump. It's a bit cramped but I'd like your ideas on the fixings to the very old stonework. I thought the main ought to be kept out of the water, but I'm not sure.

George. OK. Let's go - I'll finish the beer when we get back - strong stuff, though.

Janet. Yeah. Take courage, as they say, and drink down all unkindness.

George. Really, you must cut down on this quoting. I doubt that many in East Africa will recognize it.

Janet. Perhaps they need a bit of practice. Now, there's an idea; put on a play for the locals - by the locals.

George.   Come on. Let's get this inspection over; I'm getting dry, but fill me with the old familiar juice I might recover bye and bye.

Janet.   Sir, sir, now you're doing it. Where's that come from?

George.   No matter, come on. Got some boots? Good, thanks - *he puts them on and they set off.*

* * * * *

Back at the pump station site, where the weather is cold and there have been heavy snow falls. In his office, John Jewel is typing when the site inspector enters.

Alec.   Sir, Flash Harry has ordered the dozer driver to back-fill with snow.

Jewel.   What, the main excavation? - *Alec nods* - Go at once to see that the dozer stops. I'll see the Agent now. The man must be mad.

Both leave at a rush, Alec to the excavation, Jewel to the Agent's office where he knocks loudly and enters without invitation.

Agent.   Oh. It's you, John; what's the panic?

Jewel.   Ted. Your idiot contracts' manager has just ordered your dozer to back-fill with snow.

Agent.   What, the main excavation?

Jewel.	Yes. I've sent Alec to stop it, but you must do something to back me up or the sides could collapse.
Agent.	Of course - *he gets up, but sits down again as a very angry Flash Harry enters* -
Flash.	That bloody inspector has cancelled my order to get all that snow out of the way.
Jewel.	Yes, I told him to.
Flash.	You can't do that. It's temporary works and not your damned business.
Jewel.	Oh. Yes it is. Ted, please tell him.
Agent.	Look, Mr Smart, I know it's your first time down here, but that excavation is 50 feet deep and the bottom 30 feet is blue lias with a very steep face. If it gets persistently wet, it tends to lose strength and the whole lot could come down and take weeks to clear away before we could continue with the permanent work. So, John Jewel, here, who is the resident engineer, has every right to be concerned.
Flash.	Oh. Has he? And what's all this Ted and John thing?
Agent.	We have a good working relationship here and go formal when there's a meeting and so on - or argument.

Flash. Well he can't start ordering me about, the young whippersnapper.

Jewel. I think I'll bow out, now, for the sake of contractual harmony - show him Clauses 8 and 13(2). - *he leaves quickly shutting the door very carefully* -

Agent. OK. Let's calm down - I'll order some tea. - *opens door and shouts for tea* -

Flash. *(sitting down).* Well, I'm sorry; I didn't know, but I'm not taking this from that RE, I'll bet he hasn't got the authority.

Agent. You're probably right in theory. He's not the Engineer's Representative with Clause 2 duties, but delay could have been dangerous while he phoned his HO for instructions. Nuff said, and no harm done to the works. - *Flash simmers down* -

Flash. I think you'd better fill me in on the job before I make another balls up.

Agent. Well, it's like this .....

Back in his office, Jewel waits for Alec to report, which he does without wasting time.

Jewel. Come in Alec and tell me what happened.

Alec. Well, I told the driver to stop and he stopped, then this toff bloke comes across and tells him to

	start again. The driver asks the toff bloke who the hell he is and the toff says he's the new contracts' manager and the driver should do what he says. Anyroads, the dozer was pretty bogged down and I suggested, polite like, that the toff go and have a word with the Agent. 'You're dead right I will' he says and storms off as fast as the mud and snow would let him.
Jewel.	Good. Well done. There's been a bit of an up and a down with the Agent, and things will begin to simmer down, but this is not going to help getting about the site. We must make sure any snow melt that gets into the excavation is pumped out.
Alec.	Yes. I had a word with the General on the way back and he said he'd check the pumps down below and make sure drainage channels are clear. Funny thing about this mud, though. While I was with the General, he'd been watching two men who had walked right round the site once, squelching almost up to their knees and keeping their boots on with difficulty, carrying a ladder. As they started on the second round, the General told them to keep walking, but up to the office and pick up their cards or words to that effect.
Jewel.	*laughs* Makes a good story. - Now the Council's Assistant Chief Engineer has rung up saying he wants to see me - he's due any moment. If you could rustle up a cup or two, in wouldn't do any harm.

A few minutes later, there is a brisk knock.

Jewel.   Come in, sir. We've got a cup of tea waiting for you.

ACE.   Thanks. Not very clement weather, is it?

Jewel.   No. Please sit down, and what can I do for you?

ACE.   Well, I'll come to the point. You know the invitation out to tender for the culvert lining.

Jewel.   Yes. It's to be a nominated sub-contract.

ACE.   Yes, I know that, whatever it means, but we know one of the tenderers who does a lot of local work, very skilled in plastering and rendering and we want him to get the job.

Jewel.   Well, if his tender is the lowest, he'll certainly be considered, depending, I suppose, on his experience with grano - that is granolithic rendering.

ACE.   Anyhow, you'll do your best to see he gets the job.

Jewel.   I'm sorry, you have to understand that I have no authority in this matter. It's up to the Engineer.

ACE.   You've got my authority.

Jewel.   But, you see, I can only take instructions from the Engineer, Noplay & Partners.

ACE.   You just look at who signs your pay-checks.

Jewel.   I may be a bit dim, but I can't see how that makes any difference. Why don't you take it up with Sir Triard?

ACE.   I think you'll need to grow up more quickly, if you're to get on.

Jewel.   Yes, I know I am rather inexperienced and that's why I'd prefer it if you went higher up.

ACE.   So that's that. - *he puts down his cup and leaves shutting the door none too gently -*

* * * * *

Although the tunnel is part of the overall drainage scheme of which the pump station is an important part, it is being built under a separate contract which, nevertheless, Jewel has to supervise. At the top of a shaft in the road Jewel and the contractor's site engineer, Mackilroy, are setting a plumb line down the shaft.

Mackilroy. It's rather a long plumb, and I have had difficulty in damping the swing. Did you ever see that undamped one in the National Science Museum? It never seemed to stop - something to do with the earth's revolution, I suppose. Anyhow, I have put the lead weight into an oil bath at the bottom of the shaft, which seems to have done the trick.

Jewel.   As long as we don't touch the line on the way down. What sort of a base line will you get?

Mackilroy. It won't be too bad. We've cut a 6ft. adit, segmented - that's three rings - It should be enough. Anyhow, I bet you we break through not more than a half inch off-line.

Jewel. How much?

Mackilroy. A pint; do you?

Jewel. Done. But don't you need two wires to sight through.- *they take a sight through the line on a distant mark and prepare to carry the theodolite down -*

Mackilroy. No, not with this instrument. We just set it up approximately on line about 9 ft away in the adit, and with this sliding plate adjust it to give a 180 degree back sight, set up two dogs in the soffit and file a centre-line mark on each. They are used for further setting out and checking construction line.

Jewel. Seems a bit hit and miss.

Mackilroy. Not on your Nelly, the pint is already safely in my hand.

The next morning, the pump station Agent telephones Jewel:

Agent. Morning John, I think I've got something which may interest you - No, it's not like that. Look, you know that local tenderer for the grano rendering? Well, he's coming to see me. Why not go into the pay clerk's room and listen through the wall? But

	get a move on, I can see his car on the access road. *- the Agent puts the phone down and waits - knocks on the door -* Come in. Oh. Hello, it's you. Good morning.
Plasterer.	Yes. Hi. I've just dropped by to see if there's any news on my tender. The Assistant Chief Engineer thought it might be a good thing to show interest.
Agent.	Not yet, I'm afraid. There were quite a few to look at, and the Engineer will be seeking details of relevant experience from firms in the running. I would expect the first three.
Plasterer.	Good, because I got an enquiry - means I'm still in the running. Anyhow, you'll put in a good word for me, won't you, unless, of course, you already have?
Agent.	Well, I really don't have much of a pull in that way, 'tho' I can object on reasonable grounds - previous bad experience and the like.
Plasterer.	At least, that doesn't apply here, does it? After all you've not had any previous bad experience of us.
Agent.	No. Quite right - although actually I don't think we've ever used your firm.
Plasterer.	OK. By the way, did you like the turkey?
Agent.	What turkey?

Plasterer. The one I left in the back of your car yesterday with my calling card.

Agent. You what? Left it in the back of my car - on a site like this!

Plasterer. Oh well. My mistake. I should have known better, I suppose. It looks as though I must just wait and see.

Agent. It looks like that. But thanks for the thought. I'll let you know as soon as I hear anything. All the best.

Plasterer. Cheers. - *he leaves and the Agent goes to the wall and bangs on it -*

Agent. You there, John? Come in. - *John enters* - You heard all that?

Jewel. Yes. Did he actually leave you a turkey?

Agent. I can't say. It so happens that my wife is having a bit of a dinner, tonight, and we wondered whether you'd care to join us?

Jewel. Thanks very much. I'd like to. - Roast turkey, by any chance?

Agent. Extraordinary coincidence, but I rather think it might be.

CHAPTER 7

WHAT, NO MONEY

Once again, it is after breakfast just before Sir Triard departs for the office.

Sylvia. Well, Triard, you are really looking much better this morning.

Triard. Thanks, Sylvia, you're quite right, and you don't look so dusty yourself.

Sylvia *gasps* So early! Is it that the succession thing out of the way?

Triard. Yes; well, more or less, but you shouldn't get involved in office politics, although I know you are the soul of discretion.

Sylvia. Of course, I wouldn't dream of it, but it's nice to know what's going on, or I might put my foot in it one day.

Triard. Perish the thought. However, the partners have agreed to promote George Plate to become an Associate. It's the first step, and as soon as I can get him moved to another partner, I'm sure he'll impress.

Sylvia. Good. I like what I hear of him. Anyhow, let me know when the deed is done and I'll ask them round for a meal.

Triard.	Good idea. Meantime, how would you like a site visit?
Sylvia.	You know I always like them, infrequent as they are. Where is it this time?
Triard.	The southwest. We've got two large contracts nearing completion. George Plate is my sort of understudy on them, and for the most part they seem to have gone quite well. I'll ask him for a suitable date.
Sylvia.	With reasonable notice.
Triard.	Of course. I'll let you know in good time. Must be off now.

They kiss affectionately and he goes off, almost jauntily.

* * * * *

In the RE's office at the pump station site, Jewel and Plank (QS) are working at a table with masses of paper, files and folders.

Jewel.	These modified cost plus jobs are the very devil to value.
Plank.	Yes; the basic measurement has gone fine. I think we are agreed, at least for interim purposes. Now, we've got the cost increases to assess, and I have tried to get the paperwork ready for you.

Jewel.   OK. I see you want to start with labour increases, this month. How many more pay-sheets have you got, and how do I know they were all employed on this site?

Plank.   It would be a problem, but you could ask to see the signing on and off dockets, and wage packet receipt notes, if you like.

Jewel.   Well, I may have to do a spot check sometime. What's this one?

Plank.   It's the tea boy's. He does a bit of part time as a postie, but after site hours, so this sheet is just for site hours. - *Jewel looks at it and does some scribbling while Plank waits -*

Jewel.   Hell. Do you realize he is getting a shilling a week more than I do?

Plank.   Tough.

Jewel.   Thank you very much. - *they go on working -*

Later, on the tunnel contract, from an open shaft at road level, protected by railings, Jewel emerges, looks round and shouts at a labourer, who walks up.

Jewel.   Please get the pit boss along as soon as poss. Tell him it's urgent, and at the double, please.

Labourer.   Right, gov. - *he strolls off -*

When the pit boss has turned up, they both go down to the bottom of the shaft. One side is the entrance to an existing tunnel, at the other is the junction with the new drive, but not lined with segments for about 8 feet, with the soffit roughly timbered.

Jewel.   I hope I haven't called you unnecessarily, but it does look to me that that timbering is a bit amateurish, not to say dodgy.

Pit boss.   I've seen better. - *pauses and looks carefully* - Come on, step back into the tunnel, and keep still - and - very quiet. - *they both step back and listen* - I don't like the sound of this, never mind the look. I think we'd better get out of this and I'll get some props put in until the lining segments get here. - *there is a loud groan, a cracking sound, and part of the tunnel roof falls in* - Take a look at that, then.

Jewel.   Thanks very much; you probably saved my life.

Pit boss.   I don't know about that, but it could have been nasty. Still, the exposed soffit looks sound enough - nicely arched boulder clay. Should be OK 'til we get the whole thing sorted out.

Jewel.   How?

Pit boss.   I'll get a gang here, pronto, and they can put in a temporary soffit while they erect the rings.

Jewel.   Fine, but there'll be quite a cavity.

Pit boss.   Yes, I'll have a word with the Agent about filling it. He'll probably want a weak grout pumped in.

Jewel.   Good, but I feel a bit shaky and would like to get out now. I suppose I'd better take some levels and lines up top to check for any movement over time.

Pit boss.   I suppose so, but I think we're too deep for any serious movement until we've grouted up, and it'll be OK after that. - *they climb up the ladder, Jewel first and rapidly* -

At the same spot, down below, a few days later, Jewel and Mackilroy are measuring up.

Jewel.   I'm reminded of Ian Wallace.

Mackilroy.   How come?

Jewel.   "There's something in a sewer which has a strange allure."

Mackilroy.   Quite right in this case. The break through looks as though it was spot on. The pint's mine.

Jewel.   I don't know about that. It certainly looks fine at this edge of the existing tunnel, but looks way out the other side.

Mackilroy.   What do you mean? - *he goes to the other end of the stick gauge and looks along the old tunnel* - By gum, you're right; it looks about a foot out. - *he puts a straight edge against the old tunnel and measures off*

	the stick gauge – Blast it; it's almost exactly a foot out.
Jewel.	I don't know what this does for the pint, but I think we'd better sort this out in my office, before I report to Head Office. Sir Triard will blow his top. Could you bring your setting out calcs along this afternoon with an explanation, if possible?
Mackilroy.	OK. See you about 3, if that's alright, because I'll need to see the Agent first. *Jewel nods and both start up the ladder.*

That afternoon Mackilroy goes to the RE's office and shows Jewel his drawing marked up with the setting out details.

Mackilroy.	Well. There you see. I carried the line of the existing tunnel and measured 2ft 6in off for the centre line to aim at, and I may say we were spot on.
Jewel.	But you should have measured 3 foot off; the old tunnel is 6 foot diameter.
Mackilroy.	But that's not what it says on the drawing, which was what I was going on.
Jewel.	But it says 6' 0".
Mackilroy.	No it says 60" – a foot difference.
Jewel.	Hah. I see. The print you've got does not show clearly the apostrophe after the 6, although there

is a faint line between the 6 and the zero.

Mackilroy.   A damned sight too faint, if you ask me.

Jewel.   Well, at least we've got an explanation, but I don't know what you'll be required to do about it.

Mackilroy.   Whatever it is, it'll be an extra.

Jewel.   How come? You're responsible for the setting out.

Mackilroy.   According to the information supplied.

Jewel.   It'll certainly be interesting to see what comes down from on high.

Mackilroy.   Too right. Anyhow you can stand me my pint when we knock off.

Jewel.   The hell with that. Stand you a pint for being 6 inches out? You must be joking.

Mackilroy.   The bet was not about being off line it was about driving as set out.

Jewel.   Well half a pint then?

Mackilroy.   OK, OK. See you at the King's Arms about 6 o'clock.

Jewel.   You don't mean five foot six o'clock by any chance
– Mackilroy rolls up the drawing and goes with a scowl –

The problem has been reported to Sir Triard, who thinks about it and then telephones the City Engineer.

Triard. Please put me through to Mr Gidrock - - - Ah. Mr Gidrock, Glad to have caught you. I hope I'm not interrupting anything important? Good, well two things. Firstly, you know I wrote to you about the tunnel misalignment. - - - Yes 6 inches out on the centre line.. Did you go and have a look? - - - Good, what do you think? You'd be in the right to order a realignment , and it would be a long job and a messy one, too, including contractually, not to mention the roof fall - - - Well, frankly, I don't think it's worth setting progress back so much. The access shaft is 6 foot wide at the base, and I think that the off-centre can be smoothed out. What's that? - - - so that the shit will come down maybe with a wee bit rumble, you say. - *he laughs heartily* - Quite right. Just what I think, and a very small rumble at that. You agree that I should instruct the contractor to do some smoothing? - - - Good, I'll get George Plate to sort out what to do. - - - Thank you very much. It's been a bit of a worry. - - - What? Oh. The second thing. I'm thinking of making a site visit now that both contracts' work is nearing completion - sort of show the flag and all that and try to tie up any nasties which may be in the background. - - - Right. I thought of entertaining our site staff to lunch and the Site Agent, and perhaps Contract Manager, and wonder whether you'd care to join us? - - - Good. I'll get my secretary to liaise with yours and with the site to sort out a suitable date - - - Good. Well I look forward to seeing you there. *- he puts the phone down and sighs with relief -*

* * * * *

Sir Triard finds time to keep up-to-date with water treatment technology and joins an Institution's arranged tour of an underground water treatment works. Pipes, valves, switchgear and cables are everywhere, overhead and on the walls. The operations engineer shows the group of fairly elderly engineers over the works. He pauses at a particularly impressive section of pipework.

Engineer. Well, gentlemen, we'll stop here for a moment. As you saw at the intake, the raw water has been dosed with finely divided haematite, and had its pH adjusted so that the haematite adsorbs unwanted content of the raw water.

Triard. Including manganese?

Engineer. No, unfortunately it doesn't but, fortunately, it's not a problem in this raw water. I should say at this stage, that the process is not suitable for heavily buffered water.
To continue - the mixture has to be conveyed to the settling tank where the water's pH is adjusted back to normal, and the adsorbed gunge is released, leaving the haematite free for reuse.

Triard. So, what's the bye-product?

Engineer. Just salt, common salt – much more friendly than the more usual iron salts.

Triard. Sorry, to keep up these questions, but, as I remember, haematite is very dense, even if finely divided. Doesn't it fall out and cause blockages?

Engineer. Good question, sir. It was one of the bigger problems we had to solve. But you see this delivery pipe, here, has large elements surrounding it at frequent intervals. They are strong electro-magnets. By the way, I hope none of you has a pace-maker? They could be affected.

Triard *sotto* Now he tells us – bit late in the day – what?

The tour continues.

* * * * *

George Plate goes south west from his visit to the brewery and enters the RE's office at the pump station site to join the Agent (Mr Robinson) and Jewel.

George. So, Mr Robinson, all seems to be going to plan. The culvert is nearly at the outfall, the pump station's below ground work is complete and the superstructure has started. Well done.

Jewel. And Hutton's out.

George. And what the devil do you mean by that?

Jewel.	Sorry, sir, but during the commentary on the last test, the new commentator started by saying 'Well, Hutton looks set for his century - Oh. He's out. Clean bowled'.
George.	I didn't know you were superstitious. No matter. Yes, Mr Robinson?
Agent.	Thank you Mr Plate. Yes, on the whole, things have gone well after last year's awful weather. The winter has not been too bad after we got rid of the snow, and much of the remaining work is more or less under cover. - *there's a loud knock at the door -*
Jewel.	Oh. Hello, Alec. What's up?
Alec.	Bad news, I'm sorry to say. We've had an exceptional tide which over-topped the outfall, and the coffer burst outwards.
George.	*sotto* Hutton's out.
Agent.	Oh! No! Forgive me, Mr Plate, I'd better go and see what the damage is.
Jewel.	Thanks Alec, I think you'd better go with him. Here, take my camera. - *they both leave -* It's unbelievable. I and the site engineer examined closely the design of the temporary works. But they were all against collapsing inwards. I think there was at least 6 inches free-board above highest recorded flood. However, the permanent

	work is largely complete; it's mostly the junction with the culvert still to be done.
George.	So, Jonah Jewel, with luck, not too much of a hold-up. We'll need to consider what to do with the parts of the piles that were to be left in place. I'll think about it. It's early stages, but it looks as though the persistent south-westerly gales have built up the tide level a bit and combined with a lot of fresh from storms upstream have caused the problem. Come to think of it, I'll have to consider calling you Jonah - after this AND the tunnel collapse.
Jewel.	Please, don't, sir. Anyhow, I suppose, there may have been a consequential effect on the bore.
George.	Yes. There's that to consider. I don't know what hydrographical info is available, although not, I think, a matter for us at this stage. There does not seem to be much room for a claim, except perhaps for an extension of time, if applicable. It's not on the critical path, is it?
Jewel.	Not at present, anyway. ... George, while we're alone, could I have a word?
George.	Of, course. What's the problem?
Jewel.	It's that I've just discovered I'm getting a shilling a week less than the tea boy. It doesn't seem right, does it? So I wrote to Sir Triard.

George.   And what did he say?

Jewel.   He wrote saying that perhaps the tea boy was more valuable to the site, but he'd think about it.

George.   He does seem to be lightening up a bit these days. Anyhow, there's a general salary review at the end of June to cope with all this inflation. Why not leave it 'til then rather than high-horsing it now? He's always been very fair to staff.

Jewel.   Thanks, George, I was in three minds what to do.

George.   Good. Now what's the programme?

Jewel.   We have a meeting this afternoon with the tunnel contractor. He has a problem which I don't think is in my power to solve.

George.   Well I hope it's in mine. Let's get some lunch and you can tell me about it over a pint.

After lunch, another meeting takes place in the RE's office, this time with the Agent and Mackilroy about the tunnel contract.

Agent.   I expect Mr Jewel will have told you what we want to see you about?

George.   Yes, washers and grommets. But there's one other thing to talk about - the misalignment at the tunnel junction - but let's deal with the washers first.

Agent. It's quite simple really. The pre-cast concrete segments were shown on the drawings with the ribs having parallel sides. The segments approved by you have a slight taper which means that with the flat washers for which we have priced our tender we can't tighten up the through bolts without tearing the grommets. And this means water tightness is lost.

George. I'm not sure how desperately important that is. After all you're going to grout behind the rings of assembled segments.

Agent. Then why have them? Anyhow, it's one of the inspection requirements for acceptance.

George. Yes, I remember now. The City Engineer was insistent. I think he had in mind possible cracking of the segments, if the bolts and nuts did not fit sweetly. Well, what do you propose?

Agent. We've thought about it quite a bit and suggest that tapered washers would be the best with a tell-tale lug to make sure they are the right way up.

George. Seems OK to me; go ahead.

Agent. But, Mr Plate, there's a little matter of extra cost.

George. Is that so? How much is involved?

Agent. Difficult to assess unless it is related to the number of washers. On that basis we are willing

	to accept the minimum possible increase of a farthing a washer.
George.	Seems reasonable, at one level, anyway. I'd like to see the manufacturer's costing.
Agent.	That will be arranged.
George.	*sotto* Doubtless. - *aloud* - Now to the other matter. I have been advised that the Engineer and the City Engineer are agreed to let you off the hook and to permit a smoothing of the junction. There are several aspects to consider, not least that not only are the sides out of line but so are the soffits. It is important that the soffit junction is formed carefully. Can you prepare a proposal and method of working for me to study, say, early next week, for completion before the planned visit to site of Sir Triard and Mr Gidrock?
Agent.	Yes. I can do that, and if you agree with the proposals I can get the work done within about 6 further days. Will that be in time?
George.	Yes, that will be fine and leave a few days spare for Sir Triard's visit with the City Engineer.
Agent.	Give us a few days warning so that I can get the access cleaned up and ladders fixed and some lighting.
George.	Yes, Mr Jewel will let you know in good time. Meantime, I was disturbed to hear of the roof fall

	and would like to thank you and the pit boss for his timely - and competent - warning.
Agent.	Yes, I will and thank you. We were very lucky to get him. Good experience in that position is vital. He used to work in the mines, at the coal face, for many years, but could see trouble coming and left before it did. Lost out on redundancy payment, I suppose, but better to have a job than be chucked out.
George.	Yes, funny how things work out. Well, I've got other things to do, so forgive me if I kick you out softly.
Agent.	Funny way to put it.
George.	Sorry. It's the translation back into English of the Swahili translation from English of part of the <u>nunc dimittis</u> Now lettest thou thy servant depart in peace. Be seeing you - *they shake hands and the Agent and Mackilroy leave* - Another funny thing, John, I've just had a nasty thought. How many holes per segment are there, how many segments per ring and how many rings in all? Might add up to a tidy sum at a farthing each.
Jewel.	I'll work at it.

Another time in the RE's office, Alec has just made tea.

Jewel.	Thanks, Alec, that went down very nicely, not to mention your wife's cake. Good cook.

Alec. Yes, but she always gives me too much. She thinks my site work is very demanding physically; but I'm getting too heavy, especially stomach wise.

Jewel. Well I've got something for you too. But first, how do you think the new General Foreman is getting on?

Alec. Difficult to say at this stage, but he doesn't impress me. I gather he was a bricky by trade. He wanders round the site a lot with a drawing under his arm, which I've never seen him look at. At least, you always know where he is. There's always a halo of flies over his head. God knows what he puts on it.

Jewel. In that case, could you go down to the pump station and check that the box-outs for precast concrete entrance columns are in the right place, before they concrete the floor there.

Alec goes down to the pump station. At ground level a floor slab is reinforced and ready for concrete; the rest of the floor is finished. The General Foreman, with the drawing under his arm and a halo of flies above his head is lurking behind a column wiping spotlessly clean hands on spotless 'oily waste'. Alec is looking at the reinforcement, and looks for the General Forman, spots him and shouts.

Alec. General - a word, please - come on over here - I can see you. - *the General Foreman comes forward -*

General. What do you want, Alec?

Alec.   Mr Jewel asked me to make sure that you get the box-outs in the right place - for the columns - you know. But they are not here.

General.   Yes, Alec, I was just thinking about them. I'll have a word with the steel fixer - *unrolls his drawing and looks at it* - Hey! You.

Steelfixer.   What me, General? - *he approaches* - What's to do, then?

General.   I see you haven't put the box-outs in place for the entrance columns.

Steelfixer.   No, General, not yet --- As you can see I'm busy down here, but your signature could be needed. Why not go up to the stores and get them for me?

General.   OK.- *he goes off* -

Alec.   What do you think you're doing?

Steelfixer.   Just having a bit of fun. I wonder what the storekeeper will do. While he's up there, I'll get chippy to make the boxes up, and then, perhaps, you can check they are set right, steel wise?

Alec.   OK. Let me know when you're ready.

On his way back to the office, Alec meets the General Foreman getting into the site run-about.

Alec.   Hello again, General. Where are you off to, now?

General. The store man says he's right out of box-outs, so I'm off to General Trading to get some ready for an early start, tomorrow.

Alec. Good luck then, I hope they've got some. - *the General Foreman drives off, and Alec walks on towards the office grinning all over and wondering what General Trading will say -*

At the office. George Plate and Jewel finish a cup of tea.

George. Thanks, I needed that. Now, you'll let everyone know that Sir T and party will be visiting the pump station site next Thursday, arriving about 11 am. He's rather a stickler and won't accept entertainment from a contractor during the contract and wants you to book a table for lunch at the Old Inn. He'll want to see the tunnel work and tunnel contractor sometime after, say, 3 pm. I don't know what arrangements can be made for that - perhaps a tent and tea conveniently near the site. You could discuss it with the contractor, but to be at Sir T's expense.

Jewel. Can do. But how big's the party, especially for lunch?

George. There's Sir T and Lady Sylvia, the architect Laurel something or other, the City Engineer, me, you and your wife, Doreen isn't it, not to leave Lady Sylvia as the only woman; although by all accounts she is quite capable of holding her own, and then there's the Agent and the Contracts

	Manager. That's ten, I think. I've met the Agent, who should fit in well, but not the Contracts Manager. What's he like?
Jewel.	He's alright, a bit flashy, called Mr Harry Smart.
George.	Not known as Flash Harry by any chance?
Jewel.	Yes, that's the man - do you know him?
George.	Yes, very well. He seems to get on many of my jobs. Leans heavily on his QS.
Jewel.	Not by any chance a Mr Plank?
George.	Well, well, well. Anyhow, we don't want Plank to lunch; he really is a bit thick, but we might have some fun with Flash Harry.
Jewel.	It all sounds a bit heavy weight for me, but I think Doreen will enjoy it! I've not really had much to do with Sir Triard and have never met his wife. Of course, the architect's been down here off and on, which reminds me.
George.	Got a problem?
Jewel.	Yes. You can see the building work is progressing well, but Alec is a civil works man and fairly busy what with this and the tunnel.
George.	So what?

Jewel. Sorry, I should have explained. Sid, that's the building works inspector, has gone off sick.

George. Serious?

Jewel. I don't know. Here's his letter; it came in yesterday.
 - George reads it, laughs and sighs -

George. It can be. Especially with an older man; mumps can be dangerous, and his description of balls like 100 watt bulbs sounds painful. He could be off for some time. I'll have a word with the City Engineer to second someone else until we know the prognosis.

Jewel. Thanks, as soon as poss.; I've not much experience of building work. Now, I've got to inspect the old 6 ft tunnel. Like to come with me?

George. No thanks. You buzz off. Make sure you've got an escape in case there's a flash flood.- *Jewel leaves with torch, boots and note book -*

Jewel drives up to an open manhole in the road with traffic warning signs, parks his car, gets out and puts on his boots. Alec and a sewer man are standing by.

Jewel. Sorry, I'm a bit late. I've been told to make sure you've got an escape for me in case there's a flash flood. I must say the sky doesn't look too hopeful - heavy and pregnant with rain, one might say.

Alec. Well, let's hope the waters don't break, one

might say. - *the sewer man does a belly-jigging laugh* - That's OK, sir, I've fixed with the sewer man always to have two manholes open ahead of you and one behind. He says you'll get plenty of warning if there's a flood as the noise is quite something, but once you hear it, you'll not have a lot of time to get to an open manhole, where you can hang on to the step ladder if you can't get up in time.

Sewer man. Yes, we had someone caught like that once, but it doesn't happen often. But this chap was hanging on for dear life, when I shouted down to him that I was about to throw a rope down. 'Hurry up' he said 'I can't swim'.

Jewel. So, what happened?

Sewer man. I was hoping you'd ask that. Well, I shouted at him to go through the motions.

Jewel. Thank you very much. That's not funny at this moment. Let's get on with it. - *he disappears down manhole* -

* * * * *

On Thursday, it is lunch at the Old Inn.

Triard. Everyone got a drink? Good. Can I thank you, Mr Robinson, for making the tour of the site so trouble free - and interesting. I must say that things seem to be coming on fine. Yes, dear?

Sylvia. Laurel, I must ask you about the brickwork of the outside side wall. It's just infill between concrete columns, isn't it?

Laurel. Yes, Sylvia.

Sylvia. But how's it fixed?

Laurel. It's sealed top and sides with a two part mastic filler.

Sylvia *Lady Bracknell like* But what stops it from falling down in a high wind? - *Laurel, having just taken a mouthful of soup, splutters badly. Lady Sylvia points* - Look where that got to, Laurel, nearly the other side of the table. You must apologise to Mrs Jewel.

Triard. Dear lady, I think you should keep your trenchant, if important, comments to yourself until after lunch. - *Lady Sylvia turns to talk to Jewel and his wife opposite, and the lunch proceeds* -

Triard. Lady Sylvia, you reminded me of a conundrum. Laurel, please finish your mouthful. What is the difference between a building designed by an engineer and one designed by an architect?

Sylvia. So what is the difference?

Triard. When designed by an engineer the result is horrifying but when by an architect it is terrifying. - *all laugh, except Laurel who goes red in the face* -.

Jewel.   Sylvia, I think I've met your husband only once, when I joined the firm some years ago, please forgive me if I'm impertinent but he's not at all what I expected.

Sylvia.   That's alright, do go on.

Jewel.   Well, he seemed very severe, sort of humourless and overworked, if you know what I mean. But he seems much more jovial now, if I may say so.

Sylvia.   You may, and I agree, but what evidence do you have?

Jewel.   Well, that joke for a start, but when we were in the men's lavatory before getting the drinks it was very full indeed, and while waiting, Sir Triard in a loud voice announced that it was good for business, and then at the bar he laughed heartily when the beer was put in front of him with a lot of froth on it, and he asked the bartender whether it was Omo. The reply nearly creased him, 'no' said the barman 'this is a Tide house'.

Sylvia.   Yes, he seems to have put on a new life, although site visits usually put him in a good mood. - *she turned to the Agent .. and the lunch went on -*

George.   John, haven't I met your wife somewhere before?

Jewel.   Yes possibly at the reservoir site where she was the contractor's engineer/surveyor.

George.	Made a sort of survey party did you?
Doreen.	Yes. It was the plane table that did it for us. You see – *she went on to describe the incident* –
George.	Mr Smart, how come you've crossed my path again?
Flash.	Mr Plate. Very good to meet you again and this time with not a claim in sight.
George.	That's a relief, but a cost plus contract helps. Anyhow, I thought you were on that Scottish Hydro scheme.
Flash.	Yes I was, but when this job came up the powers that be thought that it was more up my street, especially as the hydro scheme was reaching the plant and electrical installation stage.
George.	I see. – *a waiter hovers behind Mr Smart* – Well what are you going to have for pudding?.
Flash.	I think I'll have the plums and custard.
Jewel.	Plums in a sloppy mix. Typical contractor's mix. – *Flash goes very red in the face* –
George.	Come now, Jewel, that wasn't very nice.
Jewel.	Yes, sorry, Mr Smart, nothing personal, but it did call for it.

Triard.	Ah. Jewel. Thanks for organising this. Good spot. I must come down again. Perhaps, Mr Smart, you'll think of discussing with Mr Gidrock, here, the possibility of some sort of formal opening in due course. I'd certainly like to attend.
Flash.	*nods to the City Engineer* Good idea, Sir Triard, I've been thinking along the same lines, and if you could fix for a time, Mr Gidrock, for me to come and see you, I'll be glad to sort out some sort of programme. You'll be laying the foundation stone, I presume?
Gidrock.	Glad to, Mr Smart, I'll get my secretary on to it, but I fear it'll be some councillor who will want to get the silver trowel! - c*offee starts to arrive* -.
Triard.	George before we break up and I forget, could you find time to drop into the office to see me soon?
George.	Of course, Sir Triard, I'll fix a time with your secretary and Miss Firesmoke - *general talk continues* -

* * * * *

Some days later, George has returned to London and is sitting opposite Triard at his desk.

Triard.	Not to put too fine a point, George, you've been very helpful to me in the last few years.
George.	Thank you, Sir Triard, it's been a pleasure.

Triard.   Yes, but don't interrupt. So I've discussed this with the partners and we are all agreed that you should be offered an associateship.

George.   Thank you very much, Sir Triard, it's much appreciated.

Triard.   It's only a little more than a change of title, but it will confirm your status in the firm and with our clients. You'll get a small share of the profits by way of an annual bonus – that is if there are any.

George.   As long as I don't have to share in the losses. No, I'm not being facetious but neither I nor my wife has any capital put by.

Triard.   Yes, I understand, but you can rest easy on that score. There's one more point; in view of the amount of travel you do, and will do increasingly, the partners have decided to offer you a car. Would you like that?

George.   Yes, sir, thank you very much, but we'd much prefer help towards the school fees.

Triard.   I'm afraid we can't do that; we're not giving money away.

THAT'S THE END